C000021707

THE BAR~~CLAYS~~
GUIDE TO

Law
for the Small Business

Barclays Small Business Series

Series Editors: Colin Gray and John Stanworth

This new series of highly practical books aimed at new and established small businesses has been written by carefully selected authors in conjunction with the Small Business Unit of Barclays Bank. All the authors have a wide experience of the theory and, more important, the *practice* of small business, and they address the problems that are likely to be encountered by new businesses in a clear and accessible way, including examples and case studies drawn from real business situations.

These comprehensive but compact guides will help owners and managers of small businesses to acquire the skills that are essential if they are to operate successfully in times of rapid change in the business environment.

The Barclays Guide to Marketing for the Small Business
Len Rogers

The Barclays Guide to Computing for the Small Business
Khalid Aziz

The Barclays Guide to International Trade for the Small Business
John Wilson

The Barclays Guide to Financial Management for the Small Business
Peter Wilson

The Barclays Guide to Managing Staff for the Small Business
Iain Maitland

The Barclays Guide to Managing Growth in the Small Business
Colin Gray

The Barclays Guide to Franchising for the Small Business
John Stanworth and Brian Smith

The Barclays Guide to Law for the Small Business
Stephen Lloyd

The Barclays Guide to Buying and Selling for the Small Business
John Gammon

THE BARCLAYS GUIDE TO

Law

for the Small Business

STEPHEN LLOYD

BARCLAYS
Published by
BLACKWELL

Copyright © Stephen Lloyd 1991

First published 1991

Basil Blackwell Ltd
108 Cowley Road, Oxford, OX4 1JF, UK

Basil Blackwell, Inc.
3 Cambridge Center
Cambridge, Massachusetts 02142, USA

All rights reserved. Except for the quotation of short passages for the purposes of criticism and review, no part of this publication may be reproduced, stored in a retrieval system, or transmitted, in any form or by any means, electronic, mechanical, photocopying, recording or otherwise, without the prior permission of the publisher.

Except in the United States of America, this book is sold subject to the condition that it shall not, by way of trade or otherwise, be lent, re-sold, hired out, or otherwise circulated without the publisher's prior consent in any form of binding or cover other than that in which it is published and without a similar condition including this condition being imposed on the subsequent purchaser.

British Library Cataloguing in Publication Data

A CIP catalogue record for this book is available from
the British Library.

Library of Congress Cataloging in Publication Data

Lloyd, Stephen
The Barclays guide to law for the small business / Stephen Lloyd.
p. cm.—(Barclays small business series)
'Barclays.'
ISBN 0–631–17349–8
1. Small Business—Law and legislation—Great Britain.
I. Title. II. Series.
KD2227.Z9L56 1991
346.41′0652–dc20
[344.106652] 90–15520 CIP

Typeset in 10½ on 12½pt Plantin
by Hope Services (Abingdon) Ltd
Printed in Great Britain by
T. J. Press Ltd, Padstow, Cornwall

Contents

Contents

Contents

Note

The author and publisher would like to point out that the use of the masculine pronoun is not gender specific.

The law is stated as at 30 April 1990.

Foreword

The last five years have seen a significant growth in the number of small businesses in all sectors of industry in the UK. Unfortunately they have also seen an increase in the number of problems encountered by those businesses. Often the problems could have been avoided with the right help and advice.

Barclays, in association with Basil Blackwell, is producing this series of guides to give that help and advice. They are comprehensive and written in a straightforward way. Each one has been written by a specialist in the field, in conjunction with Barclays Bank, and drawing on our joint expertise to ensure that the advice given is appropriate.

With the aid of these guides the businessman or woman will be better prepared to face the many challenges ahead, and, hopefully, will be better rewarded for their efforts.

George Cracknell
Director UK Business
Sector Services
Barclays Bank plc

Preface

This book draws together three strands of my life. For ten years I have practised as a solicitor with Bates, Wells & Braithwaite, a small firm in the City, specializing in advising small and medium-sized businesses on many aspects of commercial law. Over the years a number of my clients have asked me to recommend a simple guide to business law – this is my answer to their requests!

Secondly, during the past eight years I have given lectures to would-be businessmen and women on the law relating to new businesses. Those lectures have made me realize how important it is to be able to explain the law in a clear, accurate and practical way.

About seven years ago my wife set up a retail record shop with which I was much involved. I discovered then how few useful guides there are available to the busy new business person to explain the intricacies of leases, employment law, litigation or tax.

I have written this book with an image in mind. It is of a new business person struggling to come to terms with bank loans, leases, mortgages, insurances, guarantees, hiring staff, securing suppliers and customers, whilst at the same time worrying whether the business idea is going to come off or flop disastrously. I hope this book will bring some help to such people. Obviously it is not in any way comprehensive. I have not discussed certain important areas such as trade marks, data protection, copyright, patents or franchising to name but a few and the subjects I have covered have not been dealt with in great depth. All I have been able to do is put up a number of signposts and simple explanations to guide the reader through the early stages of the various topics, but far more detailed advice may well be needed in any particular case.

My thanks are owed to many people: first to Pat Martin who has typed and retyped the many drafts at great speed and with much good humour; to Alison Wilson, Fahana Yamin, Dinah Tuck, Jane Platt and Julian Blake, all articled clerks with my firm, who checked points, read drafts and tracked down details; finally to Lorna my wife who put up with husbandless or book-dominated evenings and weekends whilst shouldering the burdens of family life.

I

Setting Up

Outline

This chapter introduces you to the legal basics of setting up a business and covers:

- choosing a name
- how you set up
- sole trader
- partnership
- limited company

This chapter considers the available choices for establishing a new business in the United Kingdom. The key features of each choice are considered although other aspects of these different types of organization will be dealt with in many of the other chapters, for example Finance (chapter 2) and Taxation (chapter 8).

This book does not cover co-operatives, be they formed as Industrial and Provident Societies or companies limited by guarantee. Details of how to find advice about them are included in the list of useful addresses in appendix 2.

Names

What's in a name?

You need to be aware of certain restrictions that limit your freedom of choice. These apply both to sole trader and partnerships. Some of these considerations apply to limited liability companies too. These restrictions do not apply if you are carrying on trade under your own name and you do so without the intention of exploiting a rival trader's reputation in the same name.

There is no central register of business names in the United Kingdom where you can check if the name you have chosen is not already in use. There was one but it was abolished in 1982. Coining an original name is becoming increasingly difficult as so many businesses have been established and so many of the available words and titles have been taken up already. It is important to be aware of this, as if you carry on trade under the name of an existing business you may find yourself caught up in legal proceedings to prevent you using the name (known as a 'passing off' action).

You should, therefore, do what you can to find out if anyone is already using the name of your choice. The following is a list of actions you can take.

1 Check in the local telephone directories.
2 Go to the local Post Office and search through the telephone lists for the major cities.
3 Make a search of the Trade Marks Registry in the Public Search Room at the Patent Office in London or the Manchester branch between 10.00 a.m. and 4.00 p.m. on usual business days. You can search in person or pay a trade mark agent to do a search in the Service Marks Section under your chosen name. The search fee currently costs £1.05 per quarter of an hour.
   Your search at the Trade Marks Registry will be of limited use as it has only been possible to register trade names as service marks since 1986 and consequently many long-established names will not be found there.
4 Search at Companies House (see appendix 2 for addresses) to see if any limited companies have the name of your choice. The easiest way to do this is contact a firm of company formation agents.

In brief, Companies House will not register a company name if

• it is the same as a name already registered;
• it is offensive (in the opinion of the Secretary of State for Trade and Industry);
• it contains any of the words listed in the Statutory Instrument set out in appendix 3, unless you have the appropriate consent.

This may all sound like a great fuss about nothing, but it is very expensive for a new business to be hit by the costs and expenses of a 'passing off' action. Such proceedings take up valuable time, distracting you from the much more important task of getting your business up and running. In addition, if your rival gets an injunction or if you decide to back off quickly because your rival is a big company with a much deeper pocket than yours, you will have to throw away all the expensively printed materials you have prepared under the disputed name, and (if relevant) rehire the sign writer to paint a new name above your shop front!

So, take care over choosing a name. In the long run it could be worthwhile spending more time on this at the beginning to avoid an expensive mistake.

More problems with names

There are also limitations on the use of certain names under which persons may carry on business in Great Britain (this does not include Northern Ireland for which there are different rules). However your business is constituted, be it as a sole trader, a partnership or a limited liability company you cannot

1 give the impression that the business is connected with Her Majesty's government or with any local authority;
2 use any one of the names listed in appendix 3 unless you have the consent of the appropriate government department or professional body.

So if you are interested in breeding Dukes (an improbable ideal but one which might appeal to monarchists) forget the idea of calling yourself the Duke Breeder Association unless you have first obtained the consent of the Home Office, the Ministry of Agriculture, Fisheries and Food and the Department of Trade and Industry!

Service Marks

As mentioned you can register a trade name and a logo as a service mark at the Trade Marks Registry. Registration can be done in person and the Trade Marks Registry issues various publications to

3

assist the personal applicant (see appendix 1). If a personal application is too daunting you can always employ a trade mark agent but also refer to chapter 9 as the advice it gives about briefing solicitors is relevant.

A service mark registration takes up to two years.

1 Complete application form TM2 (obtained from Trade Marks Registry) together with three additional representations of the mark, each mounted on a form TM4.
2 Submit the form by post or by hand to the Registrar at the Patents Office.
3 The application form must be signed:
   (a) in the case of a limited company, by a director or the company secretary;
   (b) in the case of a partnership, by a partner on behalf of the partnership.

What can you register as a service mark?

A service mark will be examined under three headings:

- distinctiveness
- deceptiveness
- likely confusion with other registered or pending applications

The Register is split into two parts, Part A and Part B: less distinctive marks are registered in Part B, which gives less protection than Part A. Part A marks are more difficult to register. Most service marks are registered in Part B. The following are examples of registerable service marks.

1 Foreign place names, save in respect of international services. You can register Paris Hairstyles of Wigan but not Paris Bank.
2 Personal names or surnames if the surname appears not more than 15 times in the London telephone directory in the case of a local service. Thus Stalin Catering Services of Hull would be registerable so long as there are less than 15 Stalins in London (at the last count there were none).

Of course there are many other examples.

Effect of registration – service marks

Once you have filed your application and it is in the pending register you already enjoy some protection. Once registered, the service mark confers a monopoly in the use of that mark in relation to that service. Hence Stalin Catering Services of Hull will be able to restrain anyone else acting as a caterer under the name Stalin Catering Services in Hull. Consequently it is well worth registering a name as a service mark. If you employ agents it will cost you about £500. If you do it yourself you will only have to pay the fees (£163 in total in 1989).

Writing paper

Sole traders and partnerships have to comply with other provisions of the Business Names Act 1985. All business letters, written orders for goods or services, invoices and receipts issued in the course of the business and written demands for payment of business debts must include

1 the name of the sole trader or all the names of the partners;
2 in relation to each person, an address in Great Britain where he may be served with any document relating to the business (i.e. the business address).

Notices

All sole traders and partnerships must display a notice at all their premises in a prominent position. The form of such a notice is shown in figure 1.

The sole trader

You require no formal constitution to establish yourself as a sole trader. As the title implies, you and only you own the business and hence there is no need for you to regulate the running or ownership of the business. All that is your sole concern.

PARTICULARS OF OWNERSHIP OF BUSINESS (SOLE TRADERS)
Companies Act 1981 s.29 (1) (b)

Name of Business:–

The following person carries on business under the above name:–

The address for service on the above-named person of any documents relating to the business is

Figure 1

The fact that you employ staff does not alter the fact that in law you own the business and are therefore a sole trader. However, as you would expect you are not free from government controls.

1 You must register for VAT if your annual turnover subject to VAT is estimated to exceed £25,400 (at the time of writing): for further details see chapter 8.
2 You will have to keep records for pay-as-you-earn (PAYE) income tax and National Insurance contributions deducted by you from your employees' salaries or wages. Again this is dealt with in more detail in chapter 8.
3 You should register your business with your local tax office and keep proper accounts and records of your business transactions so that at the end of your financial year you can prepare your annual tax return and establish the profit or loss for the period. There is, amazingly enough, no obligation on a sole trader to prepare annual accounts. However, it would be foolish to rely upon this and not keep proper financial records!

Thus the advantages of establishing yourself as a sole trader are

- it only takes you: you need no one else;
- easy to establish, no constitution;
- minimum government supervision: you only have to register for VAT and for PAYE (if appropriate) at the local tax office;
- income tax is charged on the earnings of the preceding tax year which can help cash flow (see chapter 8);
- secrecy: the only people who see your accounts are the VAT man and the Inland Revenue. They are not open to public inspection.

It all sounds good. What are the disadvantages? The answer, quite simply, is personal risk. The sole trader has unlimited liability for the debts of the business. The law draws no distinction between your personal assets and your business debts: they are both yours. Your business is not separate from you. You are the business. All contracts are signed by you, consequently you take responsibility for them; for example borrowings, hire purchase agreements, leases, etc. If the business fails and its debts outstrip its assets, the creditors of the business can sue you and will have the right to claim against all your assets: your house (or your share of the house if it is jointly owned), your savings, your car, your household goods, everything down to the last penny. The failure of your business can make you bankrupt (see chapter 11).

Partnership

It is very easy to establish a partnership: as with a sole trader, no formal constitutional documents are required by law. Partnership is defined as being 'the relation which subsists between persons carrying on a business in common with a view to profit'. Thus partnership is a relationship: it does not create a separate legal entity, apart or distinct from the partners, so that if the partners are sued they are sued in their personal names and described as 'trading as XYZ Partnership'. In Scotland a firm is a legal person distinct from the partners. This has no effect upon the partner's personal responsibility for the debts of the firm although it means that legal proceedings can be started against 'XYZ Partnership'.

Generally partnerships (sometimes called 'firms') are restricted to

20 partners (not employees) although this limitation does not apply to solicitors, accountants and some other professionals.

Some professions, e.g. solicitors and accountants, ban their members from trading other than as sole traders or partnerships. Partnerships are similar to the sole trader in a number of ways so that much of what has been considered so far in this chapter applies to them, such as

- the legislation relating to business names;
- service marks;
- registration for VAT;
- registration for PAYE;
- filing of accounts with the Inland Revenue;
- personal liability.

Limited partnerships

It is possible to create a partnership in which some of the partners have limited liability. This is known as a limited liability partnership and is very unusual. People who wish to obtain the protection of limited liability normally establish a limited liability company. A limited partnership must consist of both of the following:

1 One or more persons called 'general partners' who are liable for all the debts and obligations of the firm.
2 One or more partners who must at the time of entering into the partnership contribute a sum of capital as property to the firm. This partner is called the limited partner and does not have to contribute to the firm's obligations beyond his original contribution. The limited partner is often called a sleeping partner as he must not take part in the management of the partnership and has no power to enter into contracts or obligations on behalf of the firm. If the limited partner takes part in the management of the firm he becomes personally liable for all the debts and obligations of the firm incurred when he takes part in the management as if he were a general partner.

A limited partnership has to be registered with the Registrar of Companies (see appendix 2) but there is no obligation to file accounts with the Registrar.

Partnerships and personal liability

Each partner is personally liable for the debts and obligations of the firm incurred when he is a partner. Because of the risks of personal liability you have to be very careful about going into partnership with someone, for you can be made to pay for the debts or wrongful acts of your partner arising in the ordinary course of the firm's activities. For example, if a partner takes in money from a customer and spends it on taking his friends to the races, the partners will have to reimburse the customer. If a partner runs up large debts on the firm's credit card when pretending to be entertaining clients, his partners will have to pay. They will be entitled to recover the money from him in either case.

Liabilities of new and retiring partners

A partner who joins an existing firm does not become liable for the debts or obligations of the firm unless he agrees to do so by what is called a novation. A novation is an agreement between the old partners, the creditor and the new partners that the new partners will be liable for the debt to the creditor and that the old partners will be exempt from liability.

Equally a retiring partner remains liable for the debts or obligations of the firm incurred before his retirement unless there is a novation. The retiring partner may remain liable for debts and obligations of the partnership incurred after he retires unless

- he gives notice of retirement to all customers of the old firm;
- a notice is placed in the *London Gazette* (see appendix 2); this may be unnecessary provided the provisions of the Business Names Act 1985 (see above) are adhered to, but it is probably prudent.

Partnership agreements

You do not need a formal partnership agreement to establish a partnership and, indeed, many partnerships carry on quite well without one. But it is not necessarily very sensible. Without a partnership deed, the Partnership Act 1890 applies. But what does that mean? What does the Act say? The Act contains a number of 'standard' provisions regulating the conduct of partners and if you reach the point of asking those questions you will undoubtedly have to consult a solicitor for advice. A proper partnership agreement helps avoid problems with your partner.

Hence if you are considering establishing a partnership you and your prospective partner(s) should draw up an agreement (not wise unless you are experts) or instruct a solicitor to draw up a partnership agreement. The precise terms of the agreement will vary depending on the particular circumstances. However, normal clauses will include the following items.

Definition   A definition of the firm's business.

Name   Details of the firm's name.

Duration   Unless otherwise stated the partnership lasts only as long as the partners agree to it. Hence if a partner resigns the partnership is dissolved.

Provision of capital   How much money is each partner putting up? What interest is being paid for the use of that money? If no agreement is made then no interest can be paid.

Calculation of profits   How are profits calculated? Is this done on a cash basis (i.e. moneys received) or on an earnings basis (i.e. bills rendered)? This is subject to agreement with the Inland Revenue.

Division of profits   Under the Partnership Act profits are divided equally between the partners. Is that what you want? What profit sharing ratios do you wish to use? Do you want partners to build up to an equal share of profits over a number of years? If so, over what period?

Accounts   It is necessary to be able to prove to the Inland Revenue the firm's profits and losses for each financial period. Hence proper accounts should be kept to show both the firm's income and payments and the position of the partners, i.e. what is due to them (or from them if the firm is making losses).

Management   Under the Partnership Act all partners have the right to an equal say in the running and management of the firm. Is that what you want?

Holidays   What holidays are partners entitled to?

Contracts Should you limit the partners' capacity to enter into major contracts? If you do this no partner could commit the firm to expenditure of, say, more than £5,000 without the other partners' approval. If a partner broke this rule the firm would still be bound by the contract (unless the other party to the contract knows about the rule) but the other partners could claim an indemnity from the partner who broke it.

Death or retirement of a partner Under the Partnership Act the death, bankruptcy or retirement of a partner immediately brings the partnership to an end. This can cause considerable problems: in the case of bankruptcy and retirement the outgoing partner will no doubt be demanding the return of his capital and of any outstanding share of profits. The Partnership Agreement should make it quite clear how the assets are to be valued. When will the payment be made?

Tax election Any retiring or deceased partner should be bound to sign an election under Section 113 of the Taxes Act 1988 that the partnership shall be deemed to continue for tax purposes (if called upon to do so). In the case of a deceased partner his personal representatives would be obliged to sign the election. This stops the partnership coming to an end in such a way that allows the Inland Revenue to tax the partners on a stricter 'closing year' base (see chapter 8).

Non-competition restrictions You can stop a retiring partner (or one who leaves) competing with your firm for a limited period provided the restriction is 'reasonable'. There have been many cases on this subject, a number of which are contradictory! It is a real legal minefield but with good advice you can obtain some protection.

Arbitration Partnerships are fairly secretive organizations and if the partners fall out it may be preferable to have the dispute dealt with behind the closed doors of an arbitration hearing rather than in the full glare of publicity in the court room.

The Partnership Agreement is a contract between the partners. It does not have to be filed in any registry where it can be scrutinized by the public. A copy will have to be sent to the Inland Revenue and will be kept on their files, but these are, of course, confidential.

Limited liability company

Everyone is familiar with 'Ltd', 'Limited', 'PLC', 'plc' or 'Public Limited Company' but what do these expressions mean? 'Ltd' and, 'Limited' indicate a private limited company. 'PLC', 'plc' or 'Public Limited Company' indicate a public limited company. All the big household names are plcs, such as Barclays Bank, Marks and Spencer, Sainsburys and ICI. Before a limited company can qualify as a plc it must have a minimum of £50,000 worth of nominal share capital, of which one quarter has been paid up. However, it should be stressed that, contrary to popular belief, a limited company does *not* have to be quoted on the Stock Exchange or the Unlisted Securities Market (USM) to be a plc.

The vast majority of limited companies in the United Kingdom are private companies limited by shares and this book concentrates on them. It does not cover companies limited by guarantee or unlimited companies.

You should also be aware that in the name 'XYZ & Co.' the '& Co.' has nothing to do with limited liability companies. It is an expression used for partnerships or sole traders. It indicates *unlimited* liability unless, of course, the name is 'XYZ & Co. *Limited*'.

What is limited liability?

Sole traders and partnerships labour under the risk of personal liability. The debts and obligations of the business are their personal liability. That is not the case with a limited company. A limited company, whether private or public, is a separate legal entity from its directors or its shareholders. Company law has created a completely separate legal personality, the limited liability company.

This was a striking piece of innovation, laid down by the Limited Liability Act 1855 and which has since swept the world. There are now over two million registered limited liability companies in England and Wales alone. The crucial concept to understand is that the debts and obligations of the limited company are its debts and not those of either its directors or its shareholders (subject to certain exceptions in the case of directors – see chapter 11).

Hence it is the limited company which is responsible for its contracts; it is the limited company which employs the staff; it is the limited company who sues or is sued. The risks of personal liability are removed; those risks become the risks of the limited company.

How is a limited company established?

To establish a limited liability company it is necessary to comply with the registration procedures laid down by the Companies Acts. Certain documents have to be filed with Companies House (see appendix 2).

- Statutory declaration by one of the directors or company secretary or a solicitor (form G12).
- Statement of first directors and company secretary (form G10).
- Memorandum and Articles of Association.
- Fee (£50).
- Form 88(1).

Once Companies House has passed the application it issues a Certificate of Incorporation. This is proof of the company's registration and it is this piece of paper which confers limited liability status.

If a limited liability company wishes to change its name it has to file a special resolution with Companies House, pay a fee of £40 and the Registrar will issue a Certificate of Incorporation on Change of Name. This usually takes about ten days. The change of name is not valid until the new certificate has been issued by Companies House.

This is not the end of the matter. A limited company may be able to register a similar (but not identical) name with Companies House, e.g. Harrods (1990) Limited. The fact of registration will not prevent Harrods bringing a Passing Off Action against Harrods (1990) Limited and seeking an injunction to restrain the use of the Harrods' name.

Company formation agents

It is possible to buy a limited company 'off the shelf' from company formation agents who specialize in setting up limited liability companies in anticipation of demand. They stockpile limited companies, all established with standard constitutions and improbable names such as Mapleleaf Limited or Datepalm Limited. The agents will sell the limited company for a fee of approximately £250 (including VAT) and this will include

- a certificate that the limited company has not traded (very important as you do not want to purchase a 'dirty' company with existing liabilities or obligations);
- the Memorandum and Articles of Association;
- resignations of the first director and secretary (who will be employees of the company formation agents);
- a change of name (if you cannot stand Mapleleaf Limited and want something more appropriate to your business).

Company formation agents are listed in the *Yellow Pages* under 'Company Registration Agents'.

Health warning

You should be very wary about buying a limited company 'off the shelf' and starting up in business without professional help. Limited companies are subject to complicated rules and it is easy to run into trouble. For example, if a limited company has only one shareholder for more than six months it loses the protections of limited liability. This could be disastrous. If a limited company omits to file returns with Companies House the directors can be subject to criminal proceedings and fines. Many private limited companies are so slow at filing returns and so adept at failing to reply to notices that Companies House assumes that they are dormant and strikes them off the Companies Registry. If this happens, all the company's surplus assets go straight to – the Crown! It is an expensive and protracted business to undo this, involving proceedings in the High Court, during which time, of course, the limited company has no access to any of its assets including bank deposits and accounts, as it no longer owns them. Instead, in theory the Crown does! In practice they are frozen.

A limited company's constitution

Unlike a sole trader or a partnership a limited company has to have a constitution. The constitution is called the Memorandum and Articles of Association.

The Memorandum of Association This sets out what the limited company is established to do, i.e. its objectives. Normally these are drafted very widely so as to give maximum flexibility. Under the Companies Act 1989 a limited company can be established for general trading purposes by adopting a standard form of objectives.

The Articles of Association ('the Articles') The Articles lay down the rules by which the limited company operates. These rules can be straightforward or complex, depending on the particular circumstances. Nearly all sets of Articles are based on a standard form set out in the Companies (Tables A–F) Regulations 1985 which provide a good working model. These rules have to be amended to meet specific needs. Your solicitor will be able to draw up Articles of Association to cater for your particular needs.

Shareholders

Companies are limited by Royal Charter, guarantee or shares. The most common form of company is 'limited by shares'. Each company limited by shares has a 'share capital' and it issues shares from its share capital to people who become its shareholders. The precise mechanics of issuing shares and the different types of shares are dealt with in chapter 2. At this stage, it might be helpful, so as to understand the idea of share capital, to picture a large cake divided into slices. A company notionally divides itself into slices (which are called shares) and distributes slices to shareholders in return for cash or other items of value. The shareholder does *not* own the company's assets which belong to the company as a separate and independent legal entity; he merely owns a part of the company itself.

A limited company must have a minimum of two shareholders

otherwise limited liability can be lost. The shareholders are vested with the residuary authority in a limited company. They are not responsible for the day-to-day running of the company – that is left to the directors. In a small private limited company the directors and shareholders are usually the same people: the entrepreneur and spouse or partner are both the shareholders and directors. But this need not be the case and the limited company is designed for a division between the functions of the shareholders and the directors.

The shareholders' power (very briefly) lies in that:

- they and only they can amend the limited company's constitution (this requires a special resolution of the shareholders, i.e. a resolution passed by 75 per cent of the shareholders present and voting at a duly convened shareholders meeting);
- they can dismiss a director (on a complicated procedure requiring 28 days clear notice to the director in question unless the Articles specify otherwise);
- they approve the audited accounts;
- they appoint the auditors.

Directors

In a small limited company the directors and shareholders will usually be the same people, but as time goes by and as shares are inherited or sold the directors can be different people from the shareholders, as in the case of big plcs where the directors will own only a tiny number of the total issued shares (if any). The directors are responsible for the day-to-day running of the limited company's business.

As a limited company is a legal creation and does not have a mind of its own, it has to carry out its actions through people. It is the job of the directors to implement the limited company's business. It is the directors who sign contracts, but on behalf of the limited company; it is the directors who instruct the auditors or other professionals, but on behalf of the limited company; it is the directors who employ or dismiss the staff, but on behalf of the limited company.

The price for limited liability

Disclosure

The best things in life may be free but limited liability is not one of them. Quite apart from the initial expenses of establishing a limited company there are other costs to bear. Ever since limited liability first became readily available in 1855 the price payable for it has been public disclosure. The affairs of the sole trader or the partnership are kept secret, but not those of the limited company.

In a small book such as this it is not possible to detail all the extensive disclosures which have to be made by limited companies to Companies House, but the principal requirements are as follows.

An annual return   Form 363 has to be forwarded to the Registrar within 42 days of the Annual General Meeting (AGM) plus a £25 fee.

Audited accounts   These have to be filed with the Registrar within 10 months of the end of the limited company's accounting period (i.e. financial year).

Subject to the provisions for small and medium sized companies (see below) accounts should include

a balance sheet
an auditor's report
a director's report

'A small company' is one which meets at least two of these three conditions:

turnover not exceeding £2m
balance sheet total not exceeding £0.975m
average number of employees not exceeding 50

'A small company' may file modified accounts. Full accounts still have to be sent to the shareholders. Modified accounts means

abbreviated balance sheet
special auditor's report

Hence the small limited company can avoid filing its profit and loss account.

'A medium company' is a company which meets at least two of three conditions:

turnover not exceeding £8m
balance sheet not exceeding £3.9m
average number of employees not exceeding 250

A medium company may also file modified accounts which means

balance sheet
profit and loss account (which may be abbreviated and not disclose turnover)
special auditor's report
director's report

Changes

- Changes in the company's accounting reference date (i.e. financial year end) have to be notified to the Registrar.
- Changes in company officers must be notified within 14 days of the event on Form 288.
- Changes in the registered office must be notified within 14 days on Form 287.
- Details of any increase in share capital have to be registered within 15 days.
- Details of any allotment of shares to shareholders have to be registered within one month.

Limited companies also have to comply with other obligations. The following particulars have to be mentioned in legible characters on all business letters and order forms of the company.

The company's place of registration (i.e. England, Wales, Scotland or Northern Ireland)
The registered company number
The address of its registered office
The company name

Note that it is not necessary to put the names of directors or their nationality on the company's writing paper, order forms etc., but if one director's name appears then *all* the directors' names must be shown. In other words 'one on, all on'.

Breaches

Breach of these requirements can lead to criminal charges and fines. For example, the maximum fine for each offence of failing to deliver in due time the annual return, a set of accounts or notice of change in a company's directors or secretary is £2,000. In addition, a court which convicts a person of failure to deliver documents to the Registrar may order that person to be banned from being a director for up to five years if he has been convicted of three or more such offences in the last five years.

Secrecy

Although small and medium sized companies can now file modified accounts, the disclosure requirements imposed upon limited companies means that many details of its business are readily available to the public or trade competitors, who can inspect all such documents in England and Wales at Companies House in London and Cardiff and in Scotland in Edinburgh (see appendix 2). If you cannot attend in person, Company Formation Agents will carry out searches and supply a photocopy of the public records for a fee (usually about £15 but it depends on the number of entries).

Complexity

Make no bones about it, company law is complicated. It has to be to regulate the vast range of activities undertaken by limited companies running businesses varying from the size of a small retail shop to the likes of ICI. In establishing a limited company the entrepreneur has to comply with company law. This means that he should take good care to get proper legal advice from a solicitor or other professional adviser. Failure to do so can result in great expense later on.

Do limited companies always give limited liability?

The answer to this question is quite simple, 'no'. Just because you have established your business as a limited company does not mean you avoid all the risks run by the sole trader or the partnership.

19

Personal guarantees

By far and away the most common cause of personal trading risk for the director or shareholder in a limited liability company is the guarantee given by that individual to either a lender or a supplier to the limited company in order to secure or guarantee the obligations of the company. This is the personal guarantee (see chapter 2).

Abuse

The protection of limited liability can also be lifted if limited company status is abused. Thus a director can be made to make a contribution to the debts of an insolvent company if it has engaged in 'wrongful trading', which broadly speaking means allowing the company to carry on trading when the director knew or ought reasonably to have known that there was no reasonable prospect of avoiding insolvency and has not taken every possible step to minimize the potential loss to creditors.

Fraudulent trading is trading with intent to defraud creditors. Again, as with wrongful trading, a director can be made personally liable for the debts of the limited company. Both these subjects are dealt with in more detail in chapter 11.

If a limited company breaks the law, e.g. relating to Trade Descriptions (see chapter 5) or Food and Drug controls, directors can be prosecuted.

Conclusion

Most people who are thinking of establishing a new business automatically assume it is best to set up a limited company. Somehow, limited company status has perpetrated a great confidence trick so most people assume a limited company is more secure, better-to-do-business-with, than a sole trader or a partnership. As this chapter has shown that is not the case.

The best advice is to take each case on its merits: 'horses for courses'. But as a generalization, given that most bankers demand personal guarantees, it is often sensible to start trading as a sole trader or partnership, taking advantage of the tax benefits and their simple structures – you can transfer the business to a limited company without any adverse tax effects after a few years. Hopefully by then your trading record may enable you to borrow money or obtain goods from suppliers on the strength of the business's reputation and balance sheet, without recourse to the dreaded personal guarantee.

Key points

- Select names with care.
- Can you set up as a sole trader/partnership?
  There is no limited liability but some advantages.
- Limited companies give limited liability but are more complex.

2

Finance

Outline

This chapter covers the legal aspects of financing your business and considers:

- loans and government grants
- share capital
- hire purchase

Loans

The sole trader, partnership or limited liability company can raise money for the business by a loan, normally from a bank but it could be from an individual or a supporter. Nearly all new businesses get some of their initial finance from loans made by the sole trader or partners. This may then help to 'gear up' the business, that is make it feasible for third parties, e.g. banks, to lend to the business because it is seen that its backers are financially committed. Equally the founder directors/shareholders of limited companies will often lend the limited company money. The vast majority of loan finance is, of course, provided by the major banks.

The borrower needs to consider a number of issues.

When is the loan repayable?

Loans are divided into two types:

Repayable on demand A good example is the normal overdraft facility; this allows the lender to call for repayment of the full loan plus all interest due at any time. Most bank loans are 'demand'

22

loans although in reality, provided interest is being paid on time and the other terms are being met, the bank will allow the loan to run on.

Term loans These are for fixed periods, e.g. five years, with the capital repayable in equal slices or 'tranches' over the period of the loan. However, some lenders now allow a 'capital holiday' during which time the borrower only pays interest. This could be for up to two years. If the borrower breaks any of the terms of the loan the lender can demand immediate repayment.

Loans – security

Lenders are primarily concerned with two tests:

1 Can the borrower 'service the loan', i.e. repay the interest and capital on time out of earnings.
2 Is there adequate security for the loan so that if the borrower fails to service the loan or breaches any of its terms the lender can be sure of recovering the moneys lent and the accrued interest?

The question of security is very important. In order to put himself in front of other creditors, the lender has to take security for his loan in the form of a charge over the business's fixed assets, i.e. fixed plant and machinery, or land and buildings or (in the case of an unincorporated business) a mortgage on the sole trader or partner's house.

The consequence of taking a mortgage on the borrower's house is that, if the borrower fails to repay the lender, then the lender has the ultimate right to take possession of the house, sell it and pay off any prior mortgages and then recoup his loan and all accrued interest and associated expenses including those incurred in selling the house. If any money is left after such a sale, the lender has to pay the balance over to the borrower.

If the lender takes a charge over the business's assets, the lender obtains the right (subject to the interests of earlier charge holders) to take the charged asset and sell it so as to recover his loan. The lender is no longer one of a number of unsecured creditors all having equal claim against the borrower's assets. The secured lender has a privileged claim against the charged asset.

Further security for loans

Lenders do not enjoy enforcing their security against the homes of their borrowers. Pictures of evicted wives and children make for bad public relations. Consequently many lenders insist on the borrower taking out a life insurance policy for a sum equivalent to the loan and some accrued interest. The borrower then charges the policy to the lender. Then, if the borrower dies, the insurance proceeds are paid to the lender.

You should be aware of your rights under the Financial Services Act 1986 in relation to such policies, which are dealt with in chapter 7.

Many would-be entrepreneurs lack the assets to put up adequate security for their business borrowing. To address this problem, the government, in conjunction with the major clearing banks, introduced the Loan Guarantee Scheme in 1981. Broadly, this allows an entrepreneur to borrow up to £100,000, and 70 per cent of the sum advanced is guaranteed by the Department of Employment to the lender. Enquiries can be made to any of the clearing banks.

Loans for limited companies

Limited liability companies have an advantage over the sole trader and partnerships when it comes to giving security for loans. Only a limited company can give a 'floating charge'. Sole traders, partnerships and limited companies can give 'fixed charges', i.e. a charge over a particular asset or group of assets, such as a property, a piece of machinery or a set of fixtures. But such fixed charges cannot be given over types of asset which keep on changing or fluctuating, e.g. stock or debtors. A limited company, however, can give a *floating* charge over such assets. The floating charge hangs like a net above the assets charged (stock, book debts, etc.): at the moment the charge is triggered ('crystallizes' in the technical jargon), the net drops and covers all the charged assets at that moment. So, for example, all the stock which is owned by a company at the moment a floating charge is triggered becomes security for the debt due to the lender and secured by the floating charge. The floating charge is only triggered if there has been a breach of the terms of the charge or the loan facility under which the charge was given. Otherwise it just hangs in suspense.

Personal guarantee

As already mentioned in chapter 1, many lenders of money to limited companies demand security for their loans. Such security can take the form of a charge over the company's assets either fixed or floating or (normally) both.

Alternatively the lender (or indeed a supplier of goods on credit) can demand a personal guarantee from the directors or shareholders of the borrowing company. This guarantee can be secured or unsecured. A secured guarantee is one which is backed up by a fixed charge over the guarantor's property. Usually this means a mortgage over the guarantor's house. If the lender seeks to enforce its guarantee it can do so against all the guarantor's property including the house. The advantage for a lender in taking a charge is that it gives the lender priority over other creditors. But the fact that a lender has not taken security does not reduce the liability under the guarantee.

Guarantees can be limited or unlimited. As the name implies a limited guarantee is limited to a certain sum, e.g. £100,000. The lender can only claim that amount from the guarantor. But if the guarantee is unlimited, the lender can claim all sums due to the lender under the guarantee. You will appreciate that this can cause great problems. For example, the spouse of a company director may agree to give a guarantee of an overdraft facility of £200,000 to the company secured on the family home (of which he or she owns 50 per cent) in favour of the company's bank. Assume that at the date the guarantee is entered into the overdraft is £50,000. Say the overdraft goes through the roof and hits its limit of £200,000. Then the lender calls on the guarantors to pay. The spouse's interest in the house will be security for the guarantee even though at the time the charge was given the debt was only one quarter of what it became. This is because the spouse knew of the £200,000 facility at the time the mortgage to secure the guarantee was signed.

Documents

Most unsecured overdraft facilities are granted with a minimum of paperwork. The borrower will fill in an account application form and agree an overdraft limit. None the less you should still be aware of the points made above.

The lender will issue a standard form of document for any loans or security. You should certainly take independent advice on the implications of signing any such documents, as should anyone else required to sign.

If a property is jointly owned, both owners should take separate legal advice before charging it to secure guarantees or borrowings.

All charges or guarantees given by individuals have to be signed by them in the presence of a witness who should provide his signature, name, address and occupation. Charges or guarantees given by limited companies should be sealed by them, using the company's common seal or signed on behalf of the company by a duly authorized person.

Government, local government and EC grants

This is not the place to list the many potential sources of finance available to new and existing businesses from various government sources. There are 300 different types of grant available. You may be able to make use of them (contact the Small Firms Service – see appendix 2).

Share capital

Share capital for limited companies

As stated in chapter 1, each company limited by shares divides its share capital into shares of a fixed amount. The usual share capital for a small limited company is £100. This is known as the company's authorized share capital.

The authorized share capital is divided into shares or units. The shares can have a nominal, face or par value (the words all mean the same) of anything between 1p and £100 (or even higher) but it is normal to give the shares a nominal value of £1.

Hence it would be normal, in the case of a limited company with an authorized share capital of £100, for its capital to be divided into 100 shares with a nominal value of £1 each. If 50 of the shares were issued, the limited company would have an authorized share capital of £100, an issued share capital of £50 and an unissued share capital of £50.

Shares can be issued part paid. Hence if a share with a nominal or par value of £1 is issued to a shareholder who only pays 50p on the share, he will remain liable to pay the remaining 50p to the limited company if called upon to do so. That shareholder's liability for the debts of the limited company is limited to the amount unpaid to the company on the shares held by him. Shares *cannot* be issued at a discount to their nominal or par value. Hence a shareholder has to pay at least £1 for each £1 share registered in his name. Shares can be issued at a premium, i.e. when a price has to be paid which is higher than the nominal or par value.

There are different types of share that can be issued by a limited company, to meet different purposes. The reader should understand that this is a highly complicated area of law to which legal textbooks devote many hundreds of pages. This is but the briefest of summaries.

Ordinary shares

Ordinary shares are also known as equity shares or 'risk' capital. The ordinary shares usually carry the main financial risk if the limited company is unsuccessful, but they also carry the greatest prospect of financial reward if the business of the limited company is successful. If a company goes into liquidation, the ordinary shareholders are the very last people to get their money back.

The great advantage of ordinary share capital for the entrepreneur is that he or she is not bound to pay anything for it, and will normally only do so when the company makes profits. The ordinary shareholders get paid dividends on their shares when the company has profits available for distribution (broadly it has profits after taking into account accumulated losses made in previous financial years). The directors decide how much money is to be paid in dividends. If the directors think the company needs to keep money back to finance future development, they can do so. And indeed, most business's experience is that growth generates its own problems – normally a demand for more cash which cannot always be financed from borrowings but instead comes out of retained profits which means less jam for the shareholders!

The disadvantage of issuing share capital is that, by selling shares in the company to outsiders, the business person reduces or 'dilutes' his or her control and ownership; to what extent clearly depends on the particular circumstances.

Shares – financial return

The shareholders in a limited company get their return on their investment in two ways:

1 Dividends (as already mentioned).
2 Capital gains on the shares. If the Company's business is profitable and successful the value of the ordinary shares will rise.

Shares – marketability

For the small business person seeking to pull in investment, he has to face the fact that ordinary shares in private limited companies have one special and major disadvantage for the investor. There is no 'exit' route. The investor's money is locked in. If he wishes to sell his shares it is normal for the Articles of Association to require that he offers the shares to his fellow shareholders, and at a price either as agreed between the vendor and the purchaser or to be fixed according to a formula or procedure laid down in the Articles. But what if none of the other shareholders wish to buy? Usually (it depends on the Articles) he can try to find someone else to sell the shares to. But who? Where does he find a purchaser? There is no ready market for shares in unquoted companies, whereas the Stock Exchange provides such a facility for shares in quoted companies.

Private companies can now purchase their own shares. However, this can be a difficult and complex process.

Preference shares

As their name implies, preference shares carry some preferential rights over ordinary shares. They are designed to get around some of the risks attached to ordinary shares; but the very nature of the shares gives them less potential for reward. The principal features are as follows:

Type of dividend Preference shares are usually described as, for example '8% Preference shares'. This means that, for each £1 invested, a dividend of 8 per cent per annum is due. Hence the dividend is fixed, rather like an interest rate. However, unlike a loan, the dividend on preference shares can only be paid if profits are available for distribution. If there are no such profits, no dividend can be paid. In this case it is often provided that the preference shareholders then have a vote on the basis of one vote per share, until the arrears of dividend are paid.

Preferential dividend The dividends on preference shares are paid before the dividends on ordinary shares. If there are accumulated arrears, those too are paid off prior to paying any ordinary dividends.

Preferential rights in a winding up If a limited company is wound up, the ordinary shareholders get paid out last (if there is any surplus after paying off the creditors). The preference shares are paid off before the ordinary shares but after the general creditors both as regards any cumulative dividends due and the capital paid up on the preference shares.

No share in capital growth Preference shares do not share in the capital growth of the company – if the company is sold at a great profit, the preference shareholders will be bought out at par. The capital gain will go to the ordinary shareholders.

Redeemable and convertible preference shares

A limited company can now purchase its own shares but it is still common for investors to put in money by way of redeemable preference shares. These are normal preference shares but with the additional feature that the company has to redeem them after, say, ten years. Hence this gives the investor a clear 'exit' route. The limited company has to redeem the shares at the stated date. To give the investor greater flexibility and choice, it is often provided that the redeemable preference shares are convertible. This allows the investor, if the company is profitable and doing well, to call upon the company to convert the preference shares into ordinary shares in the company. Hence, having had his money in during the early stages in the safer preference shares, the investor can then switch into higher yield ordinary shares at his option. The precise rate of conversion is naturally the result of negotiations between the parties and is set out in the Articles or a separate agreement.

You may be able to attract investors in your company by making use of the Business Expansion Scheme. This scheme offers tax incentives to investors in unquoted limited companies. You should ask your solicitor or accountant for further details.

Loans from directors

If you are starting up a limited company on your own without other shareholders you may need to invest your money in a mixture of loans and share capital. There are several advantages of this.

- The loan capital is easily repaid if the limited company starts to trade profitably, whereas buying back shares is more complex.
- Your loan can be backed by a charge over the company's assets. Any lender (e.g. the bank) will insist that this charge is postponed or 'deferred' (to use the jargon) to any charges given by the company to that lender. None the less, this can still give the founder some security for some of his investment.

Hire purchase and leasing

The Consumer Credit Act

The Consumer Credit Act is a misnomer. It does not apply only to consumers. Sole traders and partnerships come within it. The Consumer Credit Act lays down certain protections for borrowers or if you hire purchase or lease goods if the total credit involved on the contract is less than £15,000 (including interest). The Consumer Credit Act provides the following conditions (among many others):

1 Before entering into a hire purchase contract you must be told

- the price of the goods,
- the rate of interest,
- the total credit price.

2 If you sign a credit agreement 'off trade premises', i.e. not in a shop, showroom or finance company office (but this does *not* include *your* shop), and you sign that agreement first (i.e. before the vendor),

- you must be given a signed copy of the agreement, and
- another copy of the agreement must be sent to you within seven days, and
- you have five days 'cooling off' period in which to back out calculated from the date of receipt of the Notice of Cancellation Rights.

3 You have the right to go to court to ask that an 'extortionate' interest rate be reduced. The court will take account of your knowledge, the lender's risk and prevailing rates of interest at the date of the loan.

Hire purchase and leasing

Another obvious source of finance for the small business is to obtain goods on hire purchase or lease. There are a number of different forms of financing the acquisition of trading assets and the most popular and common are hire purchase and leasing.

Hire purchase (HP)

Under an HP agreement the hirer obtains ownership of the goods at the end of the hire period.

Each instalment payable under such an agreement is regarded as consisting of two parts:

- a hire charge
- a payment of part of the purchase price

The hire element in each instalment is a revenue expense and this is deductible in calculating the profits of the business. The capital element of the purchase price is eligible for writing-down allowances.

Leasing

Under a leasing agreement ownership of the asset usually remains in the lessor. This means that the lessor is entitled to the capital allowance (see chapter 8). The lessee is entitled to set the lease payments off as a tax deductible expense against the profits of the business.

In view of the differing tax treatments of hire purchase and lease agreements, the rates charged may vary. It is sensible to consult your accountant as to whether or not it is appropriate in your business to acquire assets under hire purchase or lease.

You should also be aware that as with banks many finance companies demand personal guarantees (normally unsecured) from the directors of limited companies who want to use hire purchase or lease finance.

Summary of sources of finance

Sole trader

- Personal cash invested as loans
- Government or other grants from public bodies
- Loans from third parties; secured by charge over personal assets?
- Hire purchase or lease

Partnership

- Partner's loans
- Government or other grants from public bodies
- Loans from third parties; secured by charge over personal assets?
- Hire purchase or lease

Limited company

- Directors/shareholders loans
- Government or other grants from public bodies
- Loans from third parties; secured by a fixed and floating charge over the company's assets plus a personal guarantee?
- Share capital:
  (a) ordinary or
  (b) preference or
  (c) redeemable preference
- Hire purchase or lease; backed by a personal guarantee.

Key points

- Where is the money coming from?
- How much does it cost? Is this the best source?
- Have you considered all the alternatives?
- What security is required?

3

Securing premises

Outline

This chapter explains the legal ramifications of acquiring premises for your business, including:

- home working
- draft lease
- lease terms explained
- buying a freehold

Working at home

Many great businesses started in the spare bedroom. Indeed Sony was started by a Corporal, discharged from the Japanese Army, assembling transistor radios in the kitchen. Starting off at home is clearly a sensible way of beginning your enterprise with much reduced overheads. It is also becoming increasingly popular with the growth of 'telecommuting'. However, there are certain legal issues that you should be aware of.

Planning laws

Using one room (or more) as an office technically requires planning permission from the local planning authority (normally the same as the local authority) although this is a provision honoured more in the breach than the observance. If your at-home business is quiet, it is unlikely that the local authority will ever become aware of it, but if it involves much noise, irritation to neighbours (e.g. lots of visitors taking up precious car parking space) then a local resident might put in a complaint. The local authority enforces planning laws by serving an enforcement notice which must specify the breach of planning law and give a time limit for compliance. If you fail to abide by an enforcement notice you can be prosecuted and fined if found guilty.

Planning applications

If you do start using part of your home as business premises you should apply for planning permission, for change of use of part of your premises, from the local authority. This involves filling in four signed copies of form PA-1 (plus an extra copy if Listed Building Consent is needed) which you can get from your local planning authority at the Town Hall; there is a fee of £53 (currently). The application will normally be considered within about eight weeks, but this varies from one planning authority to another. It is also sensible, before you even submit your application, to talk the matter through with a planning officer. You should normally telephone to make an appointment although you may be able just to call in and discuss your case.

Domestic rates and community charge

Technically, establishing a business in your home means that you should advise the rating authority. This will mean that, in addition to community charge, a home business will also have to pay uniform business rate (UBR) based on the 'rateable value' of the area of your home occupied by your business. How the rateable value is calculated is somewhat complex so we will not go into it here. You can obtain more information from your local valuations officer at the Town Hall, or from a surveyor.

Taxation

Your main residence is exempt from capital gains tax (levied on the difference between the purchase and sales prices). But what happens if your main residence is not used just for domestic purposes but for business too and you sell your house? Answer: you lose part of your exemption, and end up only being entitled to exemption from capital gains tax on that part of your residence not used for business. Hence if your business takes up 10 per cent of the floor area of the house, only 90 per cent of the capital gain will be tax free – but bear in mind that you and your spouse are each also entitled to £5,000 of capital gains free of tax each year.

Leasing commercial premises

In some ways searching for commercial business premises is similar to looking for a house. But certain estate agents specialize in the commercial market and may deal in a very small area so it is worth casting your net wide and approaching many agents: at the time of writing the commercial agents, unlike their domestic counterparts, have not all been merged together in great national chains.

Jargon

Legalspeak	*Meaning*
User	Usage
Covenant	Obligation
f.r.i.	Full repairing and insuring
Term	The length of the lease
The '54 Act	Landlord and Tenant Act 1954
Rack rent	Open market rent (nothing to do with Mr Rachman)

Commercial leases – references

As soon as you have found premises that you like, the selling or letting agent will want to know a lot about you. If you buy a freehold you merely have to come up with the money on completion. If you take a lease you are embarking on a relationship that lasts as long as the lease (and can last even longer) so the landlord wants to know whether you will be able to meet your commitments. The landlord will want to know 'how strong is the tenant's covenant?' In other words: 'is he good for the obligations under the lease?' Before many landlords will even agree to send out a draft lease they like to be satisfied on this. From their point of view this is quite reasonable. Why go to the expense and hassle of negotiating a lease if you don't know the prospective tenant will be able to meet the obligations under the lease?

So the landlord will usually demand the following (via his agent):

1 Three references (from a bank, a professional adviser, e.g. solicitor, and a trade creditor). But clearly you cannot supply a trade reference if you haven't started trading.
2 To know who will take the lease. If it is a limited company the landlord will want to see (in addition to references) copies of audited accounts. If there are none or they show a weak financial position, the landlord will demand personal guarantees from the directors and will want references on them (to check they are not bankrupt, etc.)

As you can appreciate all this takes time. Note that most agents will give out particulars of the proposed letting detailing

- rent
- responsibility for repairs
- dates of rent reviews
- rights to transfer the lease
- length of lease
- costs

If you accept these terms without objection it makes it much harder for your adviser to negotiate the lease terms so consult an experienced solicitor or surveyor first!

Draft leases – general principles

As and when the landlord is happy with the references his solicitors will issue a draft lease. You should certainly instruct a solicitor to advise you and to negotiate the lease with you. Your solicitor will almost certainly be asked at once to give an undertaking to pay the landlord's legal fees. This is a widespread practice. You can object but may well fail, depending on how buoyant the property market is. Your solicitor should try to limit this undertaking to a specific sum payable only if the lease is completed. Many landlords will not even permit the draft lease to be sent out until this undertaking has been received! Meanwhile the new business person is getting more and more frustrated.

When you come to consider the lease with your solicitor you should be aware that

- it will probably be at least 30 pages long;
- leases are tremendously varied: what is needed for a six month letting of a retail shop is very different from what is required for a 25-year lease of a complex modern building stuffed full of expensive plant and machinery; there is no standard lease laid down by Parliament;
- it can involve a complicated series of relationships: many leasehold buildings are let off in parts, this is called subletting; if you are a subtenant your immediate landlord will himself be a tenant of another landlord, e.g.

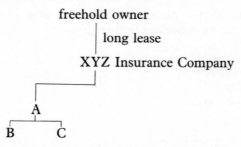

In this case B and C are subtenants of A. A is a subtenant of XYZ. XYZ is a tenant of the freehold owner. One of the reasons why it can take so long to be accepted as a potential tenant is because the superior landlord or landlords have to give their consent too! Hence, in this case, before A grants a sublease to B or C, A has to get XYZ's consent. XYZ may also have to get the freehold owner's consent.

This applies not only to subletting but also to other matters where the landlord's consent is required by the lease, e.g. carrying out alterations or improvements.

Leases – liabilities

Unlike diamonds, leases are not for ever, but your responsibilities as tenant or as a personal guarantor can last a long time. Leases are completely unlike freeholds. If you sell or transfer a freehold, unless you've been guilty of misrepresentations or fraud, your responsibility for the property ends at the date of completion of the sale. Not so with leases. The tenant's (and any guarantor's) obligations to the landlord under the lease continue *throughout the period of the lease*. Even if you transfer the lease to someone else you remain liable. So if the new tenant fails to pay the rent or repair the premises, the landlord can come back against previous tenants who have been bound by the terms of that lease. Hence many companies make a note in their accounts of 'contingent leasehold liabilities' to reflect this ability of leases to come back and grab you, just when you thought you were safe. The law reports are littered with such cases every year. When a tenant seeks the landlord's consent to transfer a lease he can request that the landlord release him from his continuing obligations under the lease but most landlords refuse to agree.

Local searches

The local authority searches which your solicitor will carry out reveal virtually nothing about planning applications in the near neighbourhood. Even if your solicitor asks about these matters he will get no proper reply. The search will reveal details of major road developments within 200 metres but not of a projected new prison in the same radius! There is no substitute for a bit of self help and inspecting the planning register at the local planning authority. If you go along to the town hall and ask about planning applications relating to a neighbourhood, the officials will supply you with the very details your solicitor's enquiries could not elicit.

A typical lease

You should read the lease carefully. Your solicitor should give you extensive advice on its terms but there is no substitute for the tenant reading the document as well, however long and turgid it may be. You must have the courage to ask all the questions that may come to mind. Usually a solicitor will not inspect the premises himself so he may be unaware from the lease and plans of practical questions such as what the next door site is used for: parking problems, access, state of repair, etc.

Moreover if you are taking a transfer of an existing lease as opposed to taking a new lease, there will be very little your solicitor can do to renegotiate its terms unless the lease is patently defective, for example it gives the tenant no right of access! Equally the terms of a sublease will be dictated by the terms of the superior lease. Your landlord will want to make sure you are bound by very similar terms to him so that, for example, at rent review time he can review your rent at the same time and in the same way as his rent is reviewed under his lease.

But whether you are considering a brand new lease or a sublease carved out of a lease granted 25 years ago there are several points that you (with your solicitor) need to consider.

What is being let?

Make sure the plan (if any) is correct. Check this on the ground. Remember your solicitor will not, himself, be going around to do this. Is the description of the property correct? Are the boundaries correctly drawn on the plan? Are the boundaries clearly marked on the ground by fences or walls?

Common rights

What rights are needed to enjoy the property? As the tenant does not usually have sole and absolute control of the property he needs to be granted proper rights for its enjoyment. The four most important are

1 the right to use all services in the building or premises, e.g. gas, water, electricity, drains, telecommunications;
2 the right of access over parts of the property not leased to him, e.g. lifts, staircases, car parks;
2 the right of access on to adjoining premises to carry out repairs to his property;
4 the right of support.

Remember: other rights may also be needed, depending on the circumstances, e.g. the right to use communal washing, kitchen or conference facilities.

Rights reserved for the landlord

What rights does the landlord reserve for himself? The landlord will keep similar rights for himself and other occupiers of the building (if relevant), for example

1 the right to run common services (electricity, etc.) through the tenant's premises;
2 the right to cause the tenant total mayhem by redeveloping neighbouring property without liability for any consequential loss or damage suffered by the tenant.

Length of leases (terms)

This partly depends on the circumstances. If you are taking a transfer of an existing lease or a sublet, then the length (or term) is dictated by the provisions of the existing lease or the superior lease. But if you are free to negotiate the length of term, how long should you go for? Most tenants like the idea of the comfort of having a long lease, e.g. 25 years. However, comfortable though this may be in theory, it has its pitfalls. As already mentioned, the tenant's liabilities carry on throughout the period (or 'term') of the lease. The longer the lease the greater the chance that some transferee of the lease might not honour his obligations. This thinking points to taking a shorter lease of, say, ten years.

Renewal of leases

At the end of the lease period what happens? If (and it is quite a big 'if') the landlord does not object, the tenant can make use of the Landlord and Tenant Act 1954 and apply to the County court or High Court for a new lease. The court will grant the lease on terms similar to the old one but at the current market rent. There is no question of the tenant being able to stay on at a low rent. The 1954 Act aims to give tenants security of tenure but the tenant has to pay the market rent.

So far, so easy, but as ever there are complications. First, the landlord can object to the granting of a new tenancy. Put very simply, the landlord will usually succeed if:

1 the tenant has been in breach of the lease, e.g. failure to pay rent or carry out repairs; or
2 the landlord wants to demolish and/or reconstruct the premises (and has proper plans to justify this); or
3 the landlord wants to use the premises himself.

Second, it is possible to 'contract out' of the tenants' rights under the 1954 Act. This is a very simple procedure and is used frequently. It involves making an application to the court for an order excluding the tenant's rights to an automatic renewal of the lease at the end of the lease. This has to be done before the lease begins. This gives a landlord great flexibility. It means that the landlord can then decide whether to grant a new lease to that tenant at the end of the term or whether to find a new tenant.

Tenants' obligations

What are the tenant's obligations? In a word 'many'. In detail the tenant promises or covenants to do a great variety of things, and these covenants will vary from lease to lease.

The most important tenant's covenants are detailed below.

Tenants' obligations to pay the rent

Rent is normally paid quarterly in advance. If it is not, the landlord can sue for the unpaid rent. It is always worth trying to negotiate a rent-free period of, for example, three months to cover the costs of carrying out necessary fitting-out works, etc. How successful the tenant is in negotiating such a concession will often depend on the state of the market. If premises are in short supply the landlord will often object; if the tenant is in a buyer's market he may be able to negotiate this point successfully.

Tenants' obligations – rent reviews

Nearly all commercial leases contain a rent review provision whereby the rent can be reviewed usually every three or five years. The review procedure varies from lease to lease, but in essence most provide for the landlord and tenant to negotiate over the rent and if they cannot reach agreement the dispute should go to arbitration.

There can be some nasty snags in rent review clauses; the following are ones to beware of particularly.

1 Those which seek to allow the landlord to charge rent on the tenants' (or previous tenants') improvements. If this is allowed, the poor old tenant ends up paying for his improvements twice – once when he paid for them and then by paying rent on them. This is avoided by ensuring that the tenants' (or previous tenants') improvements are disregarded at rent review.

2 Those which do not provide that any effect on rent of goodwill built up by the tenant should be disregarded. If this is not done the landlord could charge more rent on the basis that the premises were associated with the tenant's business and thus more valuable to the tenant, thus justifying a higher rent.

3 Rent review clauses which allow the landlord to charge the 'best' rent may mean that the tenant ends up paying more than the normal commercial rate for such premises. Under the 'best rent' formula the landlord can rely on an exceptionally high rent paid by a particular tenant for premises which were especially good for that tenant's business, which may be in excess of the normal market rent.

Beware too of rent review clauses which allow the landlord to assume whatever he may like about the premises at rent review, e.g. usage. The rent review should be conducted as a review of the premises let subject to the existing usage and the landlord should not be permitted to assume, for example, that the usage is not warehousing (low rent) but offices (higher).

4 Rent reviews invariably stipulate that the rent can only be reviewed upwards. If comparable rents have fallen, the rent review mechanism does not permit the rent to be reduced; instead the rent stays at the level it was before the review, even if this is higher than the 'open market' or normal commercial rent for such premises. This unfortunate block on the operation of a free market in rent levels is another reason why it may be sensible for a tenant to take a short (say 5–10 year) lease rather than a long one (e.g. 15–25 years). At the end of the term the tenant is free, if he wants, to vacate the premises. If rents are falling, the tenant could

then move to cheaper premises or negotiate a new lease at a lower rental with his current landlord. Hence the sooner the term ends the more flexibility the tenant may have, but it must be emphasized that this only applies if rents are falling. If property is scarce and rents are rising, the tenant may want to hold on but the landlord may be keen to move him out, tart up and rearrange the property and take advantage of rising rent levels to let the space at an inflated level. Whether to try to negotiate a short or long lease is never a simple question.

Tenants' obligations – repairs

The responsibility for repairing leasehold premises varies greatly, but as a fundamental rule the tenant ends up paying more often than not. The precise mechanics of responsibility for carrying out repairs is often a function of the type of building in question.

If you lease a self-contained building which is not part of an estate, the lease may well be called 'full repairing and insuring' (f.r.i.) by the agents. What does this mean? Ignore insurance for the moment. That is dealt with later in this chapter. 'Full repairing' means just what it says. The tenant is responsible for repairing and maintaining the premises (both inside and out). This covenant is wider than it may seem; if the premises are in a run down state, e.g. there is a hole in the roof when the tenant takes them on, he is responsible for mending that hole. The repairing obligation is actually to put *and* keep the premises in good repair. The exact scope of the repairing covenant very much depends on the wording of the lease. Does the covenant only oblige the tenant to repair or does he also have to 'renew'? What happens if there are latent defects which are not immediately discoverable on inspection but reveal themselves over time, e.g. rising damp or concrete cancer? Usually the tenant is liable but it depends on the exact wording of the lease! Does the obligation to repair extend to landlord's equipment, e.g. central heating, lifts, air conditioning plant, electrical system, etc? Answer: normally 'yes'.

Surveys

Hence a prospective tenant who takes on a lease is well advised to have the premises properly and thoroughly surveyed by a professional

44

surveyor to try to ascertain what nasty liabilities may be lurking in the building. If the survey does reveal problems, a standard way of negotiating on them is to get the landlord to agree that the tenant will carry them out but that a rent-free period will be given which is equal to the cost of the repairs.

Service charges

Many leasehold premises are not self-contained but are part of a large building or an estate and in these cases repairs are dealt with differently. The landlord should be obliged to carry out all repairs to the main structure, the common parts and the common services. The tenant should be responsible only for internal repairs and decorations and the precise extent of the tenant's premises should be clearly defined, e.g. the plaster on the walls is usually the tenant's responsibility but the walls themselves would normally be the landlord's responsibility.

This all may sound like good news for the tenant but it is not. Although the landlord should be obliged to carry out the repairs and maintenance of the main fabric of the building and all the common services, he claws back the costs from the tenants via a service charge which is usually levied proportionately to the area occupied by the tenant. Hence if the lift breaks down or concrete panels fall off the building, the tenants pay, via the service charge. This of course means that the ingoing tenant of a building or estate which is maintained by the landlord with a service charge arrangement needs to be equally careful that there are no immediate or hidden liabilities for which he will have to pay via the service charge. Hence you should have such buildings surveyed too before committing yourself.

Many landlords build up sinking funds as part of the service charge so as to save money to pay for regularly recurring expenses, e.g. renewal of a lift. It may seem harsh for a tenant who takes a short lease, say three years, that he has to help pay for a renewal that may take place years after he has vacated the premises, but such an arrangement is expected by the landlord who will see the sinking fund payment as a further charge for use of the premises and will want to charge all tenants regardless of the length of their lease.

As mentioned already, service charges only apply to premises where the landlord is providing services. In a building or on an estate with multi-occupiers the landlord will often be responsible for providing burglar alarms, fire alarms, heating and air conditioning for the building. He will also light, heat, maintain and clean the common parts, e.g. reception, stairways, lifts and corridors. He may provide security guards or reception facilities. All of these costs (along with repair and maintenance items for the structure and common services) will be recovered from the tenants via the service charge which is payable at the same time in advance as the rent. The service charge is estimated in advance and the quarterly payments are paid on account of a final bill for the year's service charge which the landlord works out at the end of his financial year. In negotiating a lease, try to ensure that there is some objective checking of the landlord's expenses, e.g. his auditors or accountants should be required to certify them. Try as well to have the right to inspect the landlord's payment records.

Tenants' alterations

Leases also vary in the degree of freedom a tenant has to carry out alterations to the premises (including electricity cables, waterpipes, etc.). Some are very restrictive and provide that the tenant cannot carry out any alterations without the landlord's consent. Others are less so and will at least allow the tenant to put up internal, collapsible partitioning without the landlord's consent. Some will require that the landlord's consent is 'not unreasonably withheld'. You should try to negotiate the greatest flexibility in this area but it is worth remembering that under the Landlord and Tenant Act 1927 a landlord cannot refuse consent to a tenant carrying out improvements (as defined in that Act) although the tenant has to go through a defined procedure before he can exercise his rights to carry out the improvements without the landlord's consent. If you do need landlord's consent you should write requesting it and send at least three copies of each plan. If you get the consent, the landlord's solicitor will issue (at your expense!) a formal licence for alterations which will set out the approval for the particular works and will usually lay down a timetable in which the works have to be carried out. Beware of any nasty clauses slipped into the licence that may allow the landlord to charge rent on the alterations at rent reviews.

Tenants' obligations – works required by law

Not only does the tenant have to carry out repairs himself or contribute to their cost through a service charge, he is also responsible under nearly all leases for ensuring that the premises comply with relevant local by-laws or Acts of Parliament. Thus the tenant has to get a fire certificate for the premises and provide the necessary fire extinguishers; it is the tenant's responsibility to make sure the premises comply with the Offices, Shops and Railway Premises Act and the Health and Safety at Work etc. Act. All of these are potentially onerous obligations and the tenant should check with his surveyor whether or not the premises present any problems.

It is worth remembering the following simple points which apply to offices. Under the Health and Safety at Work etc. Act 1974, in general you must make sure that

- the workplace is safe;
- dust, fume and noise are kept within safe levels;
- plant and machinery are safe and meet the standards set, and safe systems of work are set and followed;
- articles and substances are transported, stored and used safely;
- your employees have healthy working conditions including adequate lighting, heating, ventilation, toilet facilities, etc.

There are detailed regulations laid down under the Act. For most industrial businesses, health and safety inspectors will come from the Health and Safety Executive. Look under Health and Safety Executive in the phone book for the office nearest to you.

Offices, shops, warehouses, restaurants, hotels, etc. are the responsibility of the local authorities. Their health and safety inspectors are usually in the Council's environmental health department. Again for your nearest inspector look in the phone book.

So far as fire escapes, fire fighting equipment and other fire precautions are concerned arising under the Fire Precautions Act 1971, you should contact the local fire brigade for advice on these matters. They can inspect and advise free of charge as to what needs to be done.

Transferring or subletting the premises

The tenant's right to transfer the lease is clearly very important; without this he would be stuck with the lease for its entire duration. Transferring a lease is often called 'assignment' or 'alienation'.

1 To transfer or assign a lease is, as the name suggests, to transfer the whole lease to someone else. Instead of transferring the lease as a whole, the tenant may want to let part of the premises, in which case he will grant a sublease of part. A sublease is a lease derived from the tenant's lease, relating to the same property or part of it for the same or a lesser period than the tenant's own lease. In some circumstances a tenant may wish to sublet all of the premises and not transfer the lease, e.g. because he wants to be involved on rent reviews; this is called 'a sublet of whole'.

2 It is important to understand the tenant's rights. If the lease bans a tenant from transferring or subletting, the tenant is stuck with the lease. If on the other hand the lease provides that the tenant has to obtain the landlord's consent to a transfer or sublet, it is provided by the Landlord and Tenant Act 1927 that such consent shall not be unreasonably withheld.

Despite this, landlords were often downright slow in considering tenants' applications to transfer or sublet. This led to the Landlord and Tenant Act 1988 which provides that the landlord owes a duty to give his consent within a reasonable time or to serve on the tenant written notice of his decision whether or not to give consent specifying if appropriate the reasons for withholding consent.

If the landlord fails to give his consent or reasons within a reasonable time, the tenant can sue for breach of statutory duty.

3 Most leases ban the tenant from sharing the premises, so that if you wish your group of companies to occupy the same premises without going through the fuss of granting each separate company a separate sublease of part, that must be expressly sanctioned by the lease.

Hence if the tenant can transfer the lease and wishes to do so, he normally has to obtain the landlord's consent. The landlord has the right to investigate fully the new tenant. Can he pay the rents, can he perform the tenant's covenants? You are back to producing

48

references on the new tenant and perhaps details of guarantees. All this can, of course, take weeks. If the landlord agrees to the proposal, he will instruct his solicitors to draw up a licence to assign, whereby the landlord consents to the transfer of the lease and the incoming tenant covenants with the landlord to perform all the tenant's covenants in the lease.

Alternatively, if the tenant can and does grant a sublease, the landlord will instruct his solicitors to prepare a licence to sublet which will contain express instructions on certain aspects of the sublease.

Landlords are not permitted to charge for their consent, but they are entitled to be reimbursed for their legal costs and a small fee for registering the transfer.

Signs

Leases can present a number of problems over signs. Many give a landlord an absolute veto over the placing of signs which can be a very major constraint on a tenant's business. Such a veto needs to be resisted, and at most if the landlord's consent should be required, such consent should not be unreasonably withheld or delayed.

User

The user clause, i.e. what the premises can be used for, will not necessarily mean that there is planning permission for that use. Your solicitor should check that the premises do have planning permission for your intended use.

Landlord's obligations

Landlords have a much easier time. In a typical lease the tenant's covenants will stretch to 30 pages, the landlord's will usually run to three at most!

The landlord's covenant covers the following.

1 To allow the tenant 'quiet enjoyment' of the premises, i.e. he will not actively disturb the tenant's occupation, but this is subject to a frequent proviso that the landlord is free to do whatever he may

like on his neighbouring or adjoining property, i.e. so that he can send in the bulldozers next door and the tenant cannot complain that he has broken the covenant for quiet enjoyment.

2 To insure: this obligation is sometimes put on tenants on a full repairing and insuring lease but usually the landlord likes to keep control of insurance in his own hands and he places the insurance and charges the tenant for the premium. In a multi-occupied building or site the tenant pays for his proportion of the insurance via the service charge. The landlord will insure the building against a wide range of perils. The tenant should be able to ask for proof that the landlord has insured and to see the policy (see also chapter 7).

3 To repair: if the landlord is to be liable to carry out repairs, he must covenant to do them. If there is a service charge mechanism, the landlord should covenant to provide the stipulated services. He will of course make this subject to certain let-outs, so that he will be under no liability if he does not provide the services for reasons beyond his control.

4 To enforce other tenants' obligations: in a multi-occupied building or on an estate the landlord should covenant to enforce covenants given by other tenants, e.g. not to create excessive noise or to bring animals on to the premises.

Rent suspension

You should check that the lease has a rent suspension clause. This means that if the building is damaged or destroyed so the tenant can no longer use it, the obligation to pay rent is suspended. Surprisingly enough this is necessary, for in law a tenant still has to pay rent, even if the property is a blackened hole. Usually the landlord covenants to insure against the risk of losing the rent and charges the tenant the premium.

Managed workspace

Some organizations offer businesses short-term flexible licence or lease arrangements where either landlord or tenant can terminate the lease on three month's notice or less. This is often called managed workspace – often the landlord offers other facilities apart from the usual ones mentioned earlier, e.g. fax, telex, reception and conference rooms. These are charged for on an as-used basis. Such developments are very useful for the new business person. None the less, despite their apparent simplicity you would be wise to get the lease or licence checked by your solicitor.

Purchasing commercial premises

Commercial freeholds

You can buy freehold properties for commercial purposes; the market is limited and small since so much commercial property is leased, but commercial estate agents should be able to supply you with details of any available properties.

Purchasing a freehold for commercial purposes is similar in many respects to buying a house but the principal differences are

1 make sure the permitted user in planning law accords with your intentions;
2 are there any restrictive covenants which affect commercial use?
3 sources of finance; although some building societies are moving into commercial property loans, most such loans come from the clearing banks.

Conclusion

Choosing premises from which to carry on your business is a major decision. In retailing, the standard cliché about the determining factors for a successful business is 'site, site, site'. But not only the location is important.

If you lease premises, you must try to get the best deal by getting your solicitor or surveyor to negotiate the lease terms as hard as he can. But you must also be aware that many landlords, especially in a good market, are very reluctant to make any concessions at all. You should be prepared to call a meeting of solicitors and clients to discuss the major points of difference on the draft lease as soon as these emerge. This is much better than going through the stately minuet of solicitors passing amended draft documents back and forth between themselves, which can considerably protract matters.

Key points

- Take legal advice on leases.
- Do you really want a long lease?
- Have any property that you are leasing or buying surveyed.

4

Trading

Outline

This chapter explores the terms on which you may conduct
your business and includes:

- how a contract is made
- buying and selling goods
- supplying and obtaining services
- liabilities to third parties – the Consumer Protection Act and
  negligence/occupiers' liability
- shop hours

Having found premises, what next? Perhaps sort out the terms on
which you conduct your business.

General principles of contracts

Contract law is the backdrop to business life. Businessmen enter
into contracts all the time, whether for the supply of electricity, the
hire of a photocopier, the purchase of raw materials, the sale of a
finished product or the supply of a service.

Many people wrongly think that a contract has to be written. It
does not. Only contracts for the sale of land, hire purchase
agreements and some insurance contracts have to be in writing in
order to be enforceable. Otherwise an oral or verbal agreement is
quite sufficient. A contract may be part written, part oral. So just
because there is a written contract does not mean that statements
made at the time of the contract are not part of the contract; they
may be, depending on the nature of the statements and the terms of
the contract.

As you would expect, the law has laid down over the years a number of rules which apply to such oral contracts.

Contracts

So when is a contract made? For a contract to exist there must be an offer to enter into a contract (for example, 'I'd like to buy your car'), an acceptance ('OK') and consideration has to pass, i.e. some value must be given or contemplated ('So we agree. I'll buy your car for £500.' 'Yes, it's a deal.').

Note that a contract is only complete when all these elements come together. There must be

- an offer
- an acceptance (*not* a counter-off, e.g. '£500 isn't enough, I'll take no less than £550')
- consideration

Usually the parties will agree the consideration before the offer is accepted, e.g. 'I'll pay you £500 for your car' (offer and consideration), 'OK' (acceptance). Once the offer is accepted, then the contract is made.

By mail order or order by post, the contract commences when the supplier *posts* an acceptance letter, confirmation or the goods (whichever comes first) to the customer.

There is an exception under the Consumer Credit Act. For credit purchases which do not take place on trade premises the purchaser has a five-day 'cooling-off' period, before he is bound by the contract, during which he can withdraw from the contract.

What are the terms of the contract?

Certain minimum standards have to be met in contracts for the supply of goods or for the supply of services. These are dealt with later in this chapter. But in addition to these standards, businesses draw up their own terms and conditions of business of varying degrees of complexity. They are frequently compressed in small print on the back of invoices, order forms or even writing paper. They may appear on notice boards. Some typical points to be included in the standard terms are considered later in this chapter.

Standard terms and conditions

What is the status of these terms and conditions? Is the contract governed by them?

The answer is that such conditions will usually govern the contract but subject to a few basic propositions.

1 The conditions must be brought to the other party's attention before he makes the contract. Hence it is no use a garage relying on a sign, limiting its responsibility for damage to cars being repaired, which hangs on the back of the garage door and is only seen when the customer is leaving.

   However, if the customer had seen the notice when leaving on a *previous* visit he would almost certainly be considered to be aware of the notice by virtue of having seen it previously.

2 The last terms and conditions specified before acceptance of an offer apply. In the legal world this is known as the 'Battle of the Forms'. What happens if XYZ orders goods from ABC and sends a purchase order to ABC? On the back of the purchase order are XYZ's standard terms and conditions and they state that XYZ's terms are to apply. On receipt of the order ABC sends a confirmation notice, including ABC's standard terms and conditions.

   ABC produces the goods and sends them off with a delivery note, again including ABC's terms. XYZ accepts the goods. ABC despatches an invoice, also incorporating ABC's terms and conditions.

   If there is a dispute over the contract, e.g. over the quality of ABC's goods or late payment by XYZ, whose terms and conditions apply?

   This is a very real problem. Unfortunately this is what lawyers call a 'grey area'. The law is uncertain. There are conflicting views as to whose conditions would apply but the general view is that the applicable terms are the last ones despatched before conclusion of the contract. Hence, in this illustration, ABC's terms would apply.

3 If there is any ambiguity or uncertainty in the contract terms those will be interpreted *against* the person who inserted them and now seeks to rely on them.

4 Some of the terms may be unreasonable and unenforceable being in breach of various Acts of Parliament (see below).

Not every business person will need to draw up his own terms and conditions of business. It will depend on the nature and complexity of the business in which a person is involved. A shopkeeper selling simple objects, for instance, might consider a contract unnecessary. But that same shopkeeper will purchase goods from suppliers, services from public utilities, engage agents and enter into many contracts which will be subject to the business terms of the supplier, public utility or agent. So it is important that the business person has some knowledge of this area of the law.

Buying and selling goods

Types of contract

It is important as a business person to distinguish between two types of contract for the sale of goods:

1 Consumer contracts: the contract is made with a consumer, e.g. a shopkeeper sells a Mars Bar to a customer.
2 Non-consumer contracts: the contract is made between two business people.

Consumer contracts – implied terms

The Sale of Goods Act 1979 and the Supply of Goods and Services Act 1982 lay down certain fundamental terms about the sale of goods and contracts for the supply of goods and services which all consumer contracts *must* comply with. These are

- that the seller has the right to sell the goods, i.e. if the goods turn out to be stolen the purchaser can claim his money back;
- that the goods are of 'merchantable quality', i.e. fit for their normal expected use;
- that if the purchaser makes known to the seller a particular purpose for which the purchaser wishes to use the goods, the goods must be fit to fulfil that particular purpose rather than being generally of merchantable quality;
- that the goods are as described.

The term 'merchantable quality' has been the cause of much discussion. For example, in one court case a delivery of 'Coalite' bought by a consumer exploded when put in the grate owing to the fact that a high explosive charge was lurking in it. The court ruled that the coal merchant had broken the contract by selling the merchantable 'Coalite' irretrievably mixed with the unmerchantable explosive.

In another case a car which had been purchased second hand was found to be an insurance write-off as it had been submerged in water for 24 hours. The court ruled the car was not of merchantable quality.

But the obligation to sell goods of merchantable quality is not an obligation to sell *perfect* goods. Minor blemishes, scratches, etc. are not usually considered to be a breach of the obligation.

The Consumers' Association was so concerned over the lack of certainty about what 'merchantable quality' means that it asked lots of lawyers the same question, 'What can the buyer of a new car do if the car has a large number of minor irritating inconvenient but remediable faults which are discovered within 22 days of purchase?'. Answer: Get the repairs carried out at the seller's expense, however inconvenient, but the purchaser has *no* right to reject the goods as unmerchantable. Minor blemishes do not make goods unmerchantable.

The term 'as described' means that goods must be as they are described either by a shop assistant, on a label or in a catalogue. This is so even where the customer selects the goods for herself as in a supermarket. Hence a 'meat hamburger' must contain mainly meat.

In one case a car was sold by a firm of car dealers as 'new' when it had previously been extensively damaged by fire and then restored. The court held that the sellers had broken the Sale of Goods Act obligation to sell goods as described. The car was not 'new'. The plaintiff was awarded compensation.

Misrepresentation

A representation is a statement of fact made, by one party to a contract to another, which does not form part of the contract but is one of the reasons that makes one party enter the contract. A misrepresentation is a representation that is untrue. It is covered both by the general law and by the Misrepresentation Act 1967.

The law of misrepresentation is extraordinarily complex for what should be a straightforward matter, but is summarized below.

1 Not all statements made by salesmen are representations. The law accepts that they use exaggerated language to sell their wares, e.g. 'lovely little runner', 'great value'. These are known as 'puffs': just because the item is not 'great value' does not mean the customer can claim misrepresentation.

2 A statement of opinion is not a representation, e.g. 'you look smashing in that' (even if no one else agrees!). So if your husband hates the pink little number which the shop girl convinced you was just right for you, you have no remedies.

3 Misrepresentation must relate to a fact, e.g. 'This tow bar will last indefinitely'. If the tow bar breaks after 16 months, this would be a misrepresentation. Even if the seller honestly believed the statement to be true it is still a misrepresentation.

4 The misrepresentation must have been relied on to the detriment of the buyer.

5 Misrepresentation can be written or oral.

Proving a misrepresentation has been made is often very difficult. It will be frequently a case of the purchaser's word against the sales person's. If the purchaser has an independent witness he will find it easier to prove his case.

Business contracts – implied terms

The same obligations are implied in business contracts as in consumer contracts, namely that

- the seller must have title,
- goods must be of merchantable quality,
- goods must be fit for a particular purpose,
- goods must be as described,
- there must be no misrepresentations.

However, there are exceptions.

Contracting out

It is possible, to some extent, to 'contract out' of (avoid) the terms set out in the Sale of Goods Act 1979, the Supply of Goods and Services Act 1982 and the Misrepresentation Act 1967 in business and consumer contracts. This is governed by the Unfair Contract Terms Act 1977. The rules for consumer and business contracts are given below.

Consumer contracts

1 The seller cannot avoid liability for death or personal injury arising from his negligence by any contract term or notice. So, for example, a holiday camp cannot avoid liability should a holiday-maker be injured or killed at the holiday camp because of its negligence.
2 The seller cannot exclude his obligation under the Sale of Goods Act 1979 and the Supply of Goods and Services Act 1982 to sell only goods for which he has title.
3 The seller cannot exclude his liability under the Sale of Goods Act 1979 and the Supply of Goods and Services Act 1982 to sell goods that are of merchantable quality, fit for a particular purpose or as described.
4 The seller *can* exclude liability for misrepresentation if this is 'reasonable' as laid down in the Unfair Contract Terms Act 1977 (see 'the reasonableness test' later in this chapter).
5 the seller *can* exclude liability for other forms of damage, e.g. disappointment or delay, by an appropriately worded clause. This clause too has to be 'reasonable' (see 'the reasonableness test' later in this chapter).

Business contracts

1 The seller cannot avoid liability for death or personal injury by any contract term or notice.
2 The seller cannot exclude the obligation under the Sale of Goods Act 1979 to sell goods for which he has title.
3 The seller *can* exclude his obligation under Sections 13, 14 or 15 Sale of Goods Act 1979 to sell goods that are as described or sampled or of merchantable quality or fit for a particular purpose

provided that it is 'reasonable' to do so. This limitation only applies if the contract is made on standard written terms of business. If you negotiate an individual contract with your business customer, then the Act does not apply and you can contract out of these various obligations, even if that appears to be 'unreasonable' (see the next section for the test of whether or not a term is 'unreasonable').

4 The seller can exclude liability for misrepresentation, again if this is 'reasonable'.
5 The seller can exclude any other liabilities arising from a breach of the contract, e.g. for delay, distress or economic loss, if this is 'reasonable' (see next section).

The reasonableness test

The reader will by now appreciate that it is crucial to determine whether or not an exclusion of liability clause is 'reasonable' or not. If it is 'reasonable', the trader can exclude or limit his liability under the contract to a very considerable degree. If it is not 'reasonable', then he has much larger contractual obligations.

The test of what is or is not reasonable depends on the courts' interpretation of Section 11 of the Unfair Contract Terms Act 1977 which provides that the exclusion of liability clause shall be 'fair and reasonable . . . having regard to the circumstances which were, or ought reasonably to have been, known or in the contemplation of the parties when the contract was made'. The section gives a judge some guidelines to apply when considering whether or not a clause is 'reasonable'; these include the following.

1 The relative bargaining strength of the parties, e.g. can XYZ Chemicals (annual turnover £2 million) really negotiate a contract with ICI?
2 Has the customer received any inducement to accept the term, e.g. 'accept my terms and I'll reduce the price by 10 per cent'?
3 Whether the customer knew or ought to have known about the term, e.g. are such terms widespread in that trade; have there been any previous dealings?
4 Were the goods manufactured, processed or adapted to the special order of the customer?

5 Where liability is limited to a specific limit, e.g. 'maximum liability £500', could the supplier have covered the risk by insurance and if so, at what cost?

There have been a few cases where courts have considered the reasonableness of exclusion clauses.

In one case the claim was for damages for the loss of a number of photographic negatives of a wedding (high sentimental value) which had been received by the defendants for processing. The defendants relied on a notice which stated:

> All photographic materials are accepted on the basis that their value does not exceed the cost of the material itself. Responsibility is limited to the cost of films. No liability will be accepted, consequential or otherwise, however caused.

The court ruled that the exclusion clause was *not* reasonable under the Unfair Contract Terms Act and damages of £75 were awarded for distress and loss of enjoyment.

In another case the defendants supplied 30 lbs of cabbage seeds. The seeds were useless – they were not cabbage seeds. No cabbages grew. The plaintiff farmer sued for his loss of profit on the crop (£61,000). The defendants tried to rely on an exclusion clause which limited their liability to the cost of the seed (£130). But it was held that the exclusion clause was unreasonable and damages were awarded for loss of profit.

Breach of contract – sale of goods

A breach of contract is when one of the parties breaks one of the terms of the contract. What happens if there is a breach of contract? Clearly this depends in part on the terms of the contract, whether or not it is a consumer or non-consumer sale and whether the seller has successfully excluded liability.

Seller's obligations

This section assumes that there are no exclusion clauses or if there are they are held to be unreasonable, and hence invalid.

If the goods have not been accepted by the purchaser he has a right to reject them until such time as he has 'accepted' them. This is a little known part of the law. It can be very valuable! Acceptance is not the same thing as payment. A buyer is not treated as having accepted goods until he has had a reasonable opportunity to inspect them to see whether they conform to the contract. As ever, the word 'reasonable' crops up! What is a 'reasonable' opportunity to inspect the goods? Again the law is by no means clear. There have been only a few cases concerning this section of the Sale of Goods Act 1979. In one case in 1986 involving a family Nissan car, the High Court said that keeping a brand new car for three weeks, despite many complaints, constituted 'acceptance'. So if you think you want to reject goods, act quickly. There are good grounds for not having faulty goods repaired by the supplier because acceptance of the repair could be deemed to be acceptance of the goods. It goes without saying that if you reject the goods you are entitled to have your money back.

If it is too late to cancel the contract, the purchaser can claim damages for all losses naturally and directly flowing, in the ordinary course of events, from the breach of contract. The precise amount of damages to be claimed depends on the circumstances as shown in the following examples.

Non-delivery The purchaser should buy similar goods (if available) at the normal market price and claim the difference (if any) from the seller. If there is no available market, the purchaser can sue for his loss of profits on a resale.

Delay in delivery If a seller makes a late delivery of a profit earning item the buyer can recover damages for loss of use based on the normal use made of that item.

Defective quality The measure of damages for a breach of contract will be whatever puts the plaintiff where he would have been if the contract had been performed. Any loss must have reasonably been within the contemplation of the parties, for example:

- the difference between the actual value of the delivered goods and the value they would have had if they complied with the original contract;
- any fines the buyer has to pay, e.g. caused by food unfit for human consumption;
- buyers loss of profit under a sub-sale, e.g. where the seller knows

the buyer intends to resell the goods and it is 'reasonable' (again!) to expect that the seller knew the buyer would lose profits if the goods were defective;

- compensation for physical injury to the buyer, e.g. in one case the buyer of woollen underwear contracted dermatitis through the defective condition of the goods – the buyer recovered damages;
- compensation for injury to other property of the buyer, e.g. in one case game farmers bought compounded meal for feeding to their pheasants and many chicks died and others grew up stunted because their meal contained a toxic substance; it was held that farmers could recover damages for the loss of the birds and the reduced value of the survivors.

However, the following obligations must be noted carefully.

Obligation to mitigate

The buyer's right to claim damages for breach is subject to a very important obligation. He must take reasonable steps to reduce or 'mitigate' the loss. He cannot sit back, do nothing and let the damages mount up. He must, so far as it is reasonable, try to limit the damage to his business. If he succeeds in avoiding his loss, then he can make no claim. Any expenses or losses he incurs in carrying out his duty to mitigate his loss *are* recoverable from the seller even if his attempts to mitigate fail.

Buyer's obligations

There are of course important obligations on the buyer. He has to pay for the goods he has contracted to purchase or accepted. Failure to pay is certainly the most widespread type of breach of contract in commercial life.

Seller's remedies

What are the seller's remedies if the buyer fails to pay?

Direct remedies

1 If the seller has control of the goods he can exercise a lien. A lien is a right to hold goods until they are paid for.

2 If the buyer becomes insolvent whilst the goods are in transit to the buyer, the seller can tell the carrier to stop the goods and, if the seller wishes, to bring them back.

3 The seller can retain ownership or 'title' of the goods even after they have been delivered and accepted by the buyer. This requires a special clause in the seller's terms and conditions of business known as a Romalpa clause. Romalpa clauses are named after a Court of Appeal case involving a company called Romalpa Aluminium Ltd where it was held that a clause stating that the seller reserved his title (or ownership) to goods sold until all sums owing from the buyer for those goods were paid, was valid and effective. This means that if the seller's terms and conditions apply to the contract and contain a Romalpa clause he can go into the buyer's premises and seize back unpaid goods.

A well-worded Romalpa clause should specify that the goods are held by the buyer as a bailee and the buyer should undertake to clearly mark them as the seller's property and store them separately. Romalpa clauses can become extremely complex. For example, if the seller is supplying goods which then become processed or incorporated into something else, e.g. resin used in making chipboard, it is not possible to retain ownership of the resin once it has been injected into the chipboard (but it may be possible for the seller to have an interest in the proceeds of sale of the chipboard). Romalpa clauses should be drafted by solicitors.

Sue for the price

If he cannot exercise any of the direct remedies, the seller can sue for the price of the goods delivered plus interest.

Supplying and purchasing services

Supplying services – implied conditions

The Supply of Goods and Services Act 1982 has already been mentioned. At common law, suppliers of services, e.g. plumbers, builders, repairers, etc., have a duty to exercise reasonable care and skill in carrying out their jobs. Professionals, e.g. solicitors have to exercise the degree of care which is to be expected of a professional man of ordinary competence and experience. These common law duties have now been clarified and enhanced by the 1982 Act.

Services – care and skill

The 1982 Act implies in each contract, under which a person agrees to carry out a service, that the supplier will carry out the service with reasonable care and skill.

It must be noted, however, that this applies only where the services are provided as part of a business, but does not apply to services given free, nor to advocates in connection with their appearances in court, company directors or building societies.

Again one comes up against the term 'reasonable'. What is reasonable care and skill? As with 'merchantable' quality there is much room for dispute and it is not a standard of perfection.

For example, a solicitor is not bound to have a perfect knowledge of the law but he should have a sound knowledge, and where the distinction lies between 'perfect' and 'sound' is a subtle matter, to be decided on the facts of each individual case. So a solicitor has been held not to have exercised reasonable care by sending a letter by second class post when it should have gone first class to enable clients to comply with a time limit. But this does not mean that all solicitors' letters have to go by first class post.

As under the sale of goods, this implied term of the contract can be excluded from a non-consumer contract if the exclusion clause is 'reasonable'.

Services – suitable materials

The 1982 Act implies that the supplier will use suitable materials of proper quality. Again, this term can be excluded from a non-consumer contract if it is 'reasonable'.

Services – reasonable period

If the time for carrying out the service is not fixed by the contract, the 1982 Act implies that it will be carried out within a 'reasonable' time. This only applies if the provider of the service is in business. What is reasonable is again a matter of interpretation. The case of *Charnock* v. *Liverpool Corporation* (1968), although decided 14 years before the Act, is still a good illustration. In this case repairs to a damaged car took eight weeks when five was the maximum reasonable time. The court ruled that the repairers were in breach of their implied obligation to carry out repairs within a reasonable period.

The implied term that a service will be completed in a 'reasonable' period can be excluded from a non-consumer contract if it is 'reasonable' to do so.

Services – reasonable price

If the price for a service is not fixed by the contract, there is an implied term that the charge made will be 'reasonable'. This applies to all contracts, not just ones where the supplier is in business.

Note too that this implied term applies only if the parties have not agreed a price. If they have, that price is binding, however unreasonable it may be. This implied term can also be excluded from non-consumer contracts if it is reasonable to do so.

Standard terms of business

Do you need to draw up standard terms of business to apply to your contracts? Or are you happy to rely on oral contracts, with the implied terms set out earlier in the chapter? Your answer will vary depending on the type of business involved but as a general rule it is sensible to have written terms and conditions and to seek to impose these.

You may be able to use a standard set of business conditions which apply to your trade. Some trade associations, for example The British Association of Removers, draw up very comprehensive contract conditions which members then use. If there is no such trade association in your field, then it is wise to instruct a solicitor to draw up your terms and conditions. Too many business people think they can cobble together a set of business conditions by taking what they regard as the choicest morsels from various documents and amalgamating them in what can be a frightful legal hotchpotch. So be warned. By all means take along examples of competitors' terms and conditions to your solicitor for him to be aware of particular problems associated with your industry. He will know that slavishly copying them will be a breach of copyright.

Once you have settled your standard form you should have it printed. Usually this is done in tiny print in faint grey so that the terms are barely readable. This is not a good idea. If the conditions are too difficult to read, a judge might rule that they do not apply. By all means print them on the back of quotations, order forms, forms of acceptance and invoices but print them legibly!

Standard terms and conditions – check-list

Set out below is a short check-list of points to be included in a general set of terms and conditions of trading. They are not exhaustive. They merely highlight certain important issues. They are made on the basis of a sale of goods, but suitably adapted could apply to a supply of services.

General   Do they exclude any variation unless this is written and signed by a director of the company or the proprietor of the business or a partner?

Quotations   How long are these open for? 30 days? Do different prices apply to exports? Do they include VAT?

Price

- Can the seller increase the price? If so, how?
- Is the price ex works?
- Is the price exclusive of VAT? Does it include carriage, insurance or freight?

Terms of payment

- What time is given to pay? Is there a prompt payment discount?
- If it is an export contract, in what currency is payment made? This is most important as otherwise you may end up making a loss on a contract, just because of currency fluctuations.
- Is interest due on unpaid invoices? If so, at what rate? From when is it charged?

Delivery

- Who delivers?
- Are delivery dates estimates only?

Risk and property

- When does the buyer take the *risk* of damage to or loss of the goods (i.e. need to insure them)?
- Does the seller have a Romalpa clause to reserve title in the goods until paid for?
- If there is a Romalpa clause, is the buyer obliged to store the goods separately and mark them as being the property of the seller?

Warranties

- Does the seller seek to limit his obligations as to merchantable quality, fitness for purpose, or correspondence with samples under the Sale of Goods Act or the equivalent obligations in respect of services?
- Does the seller seek to limit his liability for any losses arising under the contract so that his liability for negligence, delay, consequential loss, etc. is limited, e.g. to the value of the goods sold?
- Does the seller need a *force majeure* clause, that is one which prevents him being liable for any loss caused by his failure to fulfil his obligations under the contract for reasons beyond his control, e.g. fire, bad weather, strikes, destruction of premises?

Arbitration

- Should disputes be referred to an expert arbitrator rather than being left to the courts? This only applies to business contracts. Arbitration clauses in consumer contracts which automatically refer disputes to arbitration rather than to the courts are banned by the Consumer Arbitration Agreements Act 1988.
- If arbitration is necessary, who is to appoint the arbitrator? And bear in mind that, although arbitration is secret and often quicker, it is often more expensive than going to court as the arbitrator has to be paid as well. The £60 Writ fee (High Court) or

£43 Summons (County Court) pays for the judge and the courtroom. Of course you will still have legal fees, either way.

Termination How is the contract to be ended if it is more than a one-off agreement? What notice should be given? What happens if there is a breach of contract by one party? Does that automatically give the other the right to terminate?

Governing law Does the contract stipulate which legal system is to regulate any disputes? This is very important, as otherwise large sums can be spent just deciding which legal system applies. This is relevant even for trading within the United Kingdom as English and Scottish law differs. It is another example of why it can be very important to ensure that *your* trading conditions apply to the contract.

Liabilities to third parties

So far in this chapter we have considered contracts. We must now look at the obligations owed to persons who are not parties to a contract; for convenience such persons are called 'third parties'. Consider the following example.

A take-away sells a packet of salmonella-infected chicken nuggets to Danny. Danny gives some to Smithy. Smithy falls ill. Danny has a contract with the take-away. Danny can sue for breach of the obligation to supply merchantable chicken nuggets. Smithy has no contract. He is a third party. But he too has legal rights against the take-away. He can sue, not in contract, but in a completely separate area of law called tort, and claim damages on the grounds that the take-away has been negligent. 'Tort' is the legal word for the law concerning wrongs done to a person for which compensation can be obtained.

In this case Danny would have to prove that the chicken nuggets were infected with salmonella and were therefore not of merchantable quality. As Smithy was suing in tort he would have to prove

- that the take-away had been *negligent* in allowing salmonella to get into the chicken (which might be much harder to prove than just establishing that the chicken contained salmonella);

- that he was owed a duty of care, i.e. not to be negligent;
- that it was reasonably foreseeable that he would suffer loss or injury as a result of the negligence.

Goods – The Consumer Protection Act 1987

It is often very difficult for third parties to prove negligence. To combat this, the European Commission proposed that what is called 'strict liability' be imposed on producers or importers of defective products. Strict liability means that the producer of a product is liable for any damage which is caused by a defect in that product. All the plaintiff has to do is to prove to the court that

- there was a defect,
- the defect caused damage.

The plaintiff no longer has to prove the producer was negligent. If he can prove there was a defect and this caused damage, the producer is automatically (or strictly) liable for that damage.

This is now set out in the Consumer Protection Act 1987. It must be emphasized that the Act does not only apply to third parties, although it is dealt with in this section under liabilities to third parties. The purchaser of the defective goods who has rights in contract (for breach of merchantable quality) also has rights under the Consumer Protection Act. In summary, the Act makes the producer of a product (and certain others) liable in damages for personal injury and some property damage caused by a defect in the product, without the plaintiff having to show fault, though certain defences may be used by the producer.

Defective defined

A product is defective if the safety of the product is not such as persons are generally entitled to expect. The persons who may be liable for supplying defective products are

- the producer,
- any person who puts his name on the product, e.g. the seller of a suit, and
- any person who imports the item from outside the European Community.

The Act does not apply to unprocessed agricultural or game produce. So a fresh apple will not be covered by the Act but the apple in an apple tart will be.

Private use

The Act only applies to defective products which are ordinarily intended for private use, occupation or consumption and which were intended by the person suffering the loss or damage for his own private use, occupation or consumption. Hence where business property is damaged the Act does not apply: its title is absolutely correct – it is all about *consumer* protection.

Damages

The damages which can be recovered are only in respect of death, personal injury or any loss of or damage to property. This does not cover economic loss, i.e. loss of profits or consequential loss. Hence, if an engine component exploded damaging the engine, the damages which could be claimed would be the costs of repairing the damaged engine. Amazingly enough no claim could be made for loss of sales caused by a sales person not having his car, i.e. consequential loss. There is no liability for the loss of or damage to the defective product itself. Hence, if the component merely self-destructed there could be no claim! The minimum level of damages that can be claimed is £275. There is no maximum limit.

Defences

Certain defences are available to a claim made under the Act:

1 The defect did not exist at the time of supply.
2 The state of scientific and technical knowledge at the relevant time was not such that a producer of such products might be expected to have discovered the defect. This is called the 'development risk' defence. Reasonable though it may sound, it is highly controversial, as many consumer groups consider that it puts back on the victim the job of proving the producer was negligent, which is what the Consumer Protection Act was designed to stop!

A producer or supplier cannot 'contract out' of his obligation under the 1987 Act. Accordingly, the best protection that a producer or supplier or importer of non-EC goods can do is to make sure he has adequate insurance cover for product liability.

Negligence

English law had already developed considerable rights for third parties to sue for damages in respect of losses caused by defective products, be it death, personal injury or damage to property, before the Consumer Protection Act was passed. Although the Consumer Protection Act now makes it no longer necessary to use the law of negligence so far as consumer products are concerned, it is still relevant

- for cases of defective *non-consumer* products;
- if a *consumer* wishes to sue for consequential loss or loss of profits caused by a defective product, as these losses cannot be recovered under the Consumer Protection Act.

An example of proven negligence may help to illustrate this. *Donaghue* v. *Stevenson* (1932) involved a decomposing snail in a ginger beer bottle. The ginger beer was bought by A who gave it to a friend. The friend drank it and claimed she became ill.

Aided by a campaigning Glasgow solicitor, the friend took the case right up to the House of Lords, who ruled the manufacturer owed her a duty of care to make sure that no snails were floating in the ginger beer. The manufacturer had been negligent.

Damages in negligence

But what damages can be recovered if you establish that the manufacturer was negligent? Answer: not all you might expect, and not as much as for a breach of contract. This is illustrated by *Muirhead* v. *Industrial Tank Specialists Ltd* (1986).

In this case French electrical manufacturers were negligent in supplying (via an intermediary) pumps which were suitable for French voltage, but were unsuitable for English voltages. As a result the plaintiff's stock of farmed lobsters died from lack of oxygen. The plaintiff had therefore sustained the following losses:

- loss of the lobsters
- loss of profit on the sale of the lobsters
- the investment in the defective pumps
- expenditure on trying to make the wretched pumps work
- interruption in profitability of the lobster farm

Could he recover all of these losses? Far from it: all the damages he recovered were

- the value of the lobsters
- certain consequential expenses in salvaging them for resale

All the other claims were dismissed.

It must be emphasized that to recover any damages in negligence for defective goods there has to be personal injury or damage to property apart from the defective product. If the defective product causes no personal injury or damage to property, then you cannot bring a successful action in negligence. So if you discover a defect in a product *before* it causes any damage and repair it, you *cannot* recover the repair costs from the manufacturer in negligence. Even if it is irreparable you cannot sue in negligence. You cannot claim damages for what lawyers call 'pure economic loss' arising from negligence, i.e. the cost of replacing the defective part or the loss of profits suffered because a piece of machinery has a defective component. This is the rationale for the apparent injustice in the Muirhead case.

Negligence – services

A professional may prepare a report which is then used not by his client (with whom he has a contract) but by a third party. In this case, the law of negligence applies, as in the case of *Smith* v. *Eric S. Bush* (1989).

A surveyor prepared a report on a house for a building society. The report was negligently prepared. The report was passed on by the building society to the purchaser who bought the house on the strength of it, only to find defects later.

The purchaser sued the surveyor and received damages, despite the fact that the survey had included a disclaimer of liability clause. The House of Lords held that the disclaimer was unreasonable under the Unfair Contract Terms Act 1977 and hence could not be relied on.

What about accountants? Do they owe a duty of care in preparing an audit of a company's accounts? Accountants have a duty to the company in contract law to use reasonable care and skill. But what about the general public who may rely on audited accounts before making an investment? Do accountants owe them a duty of care? Surprisingly enough, the answer is 'no'. Equally they do not owe a duty of care in tort to bankers who may rely on audited accounts when considering whether or not to grant a loan facility. This was made clear in the Al Saudi Banque case in 1989.

Getting out of liability – negligence

What about disclaimers? Can you get out of your liabilities for negligence by a suitably worded notice?

1 Back to the Unfair Contract Terms Act (it does not apply just to contracts). You cannot limit liability for death or personal injury. You can limit your liability for other forms of damage if it is 'reasonable' to do so – the question of 'reasonableness' is determined by whether it is 'fair and reasonable to allow reliance on it having regard to all the circumstances obtaining when the liability arose'.

2 Many businesses use the expression 'E&OE' (errors and omissions excepted) rather like a mystical mantra, hoping it will ward off the perils of liability, but it may well not do this if challenged.

Negligence and services – damages

Now for the really confusing part. As explained, damages cannot be recovered for 'pure economic loss' in the case of negligent production or supply of goods which have not caused physical injury or damage to property. Simple. But damages *can* be recovered for pure economic loss without proof of physical injury or damage to property if *services* are performed negligently, e.g. the surveyor who prepares the report without ever entering the house; the solicitor who prepares the will but makes it invalid by not ensuring that it is witnessed properly. In each of these cases there is no question of having to prove physical damage or personal injury; damages can be recovered for the financial losses sustained.

Shop hours

Despite various attempts to modernize the law, this remains yet another point of English law which is totally confusing. It should not be so. Citizens should be able to know what normal shopping hours are.

The Shops Act 1950 regulates retail shops and some wholesale shops. Every shop must be closed not later than 1 p.m. on one weekday in each week. Certain trades are exempted including off licences; the sale of refreshments; aircraft or motor or cycle supplies and accessories; newspapers and periodicals; meat, fish, bread, fruit, sweets, vegetables and other perishables; tobacco; and medical supplies. If a majority of shopkeepers agree, the local authority can suspend the early closing provisions.

Sunday trading

Every shop must be closed on Sunday, but this is subject to certain exceptions which make for the chaos. The following is a list of some of these exceptions.

1 A post office can open (but try finding one)
2 An undertaker can open
3 You can sell

  liquor
  meals or take-aways (but not fish and chips)
  cooked or partly cooked tripe
  sweets and ice cream
  flowers, fruit and vegetables (but not tinned fruit)
  milk and cream (but not tinned or dried milk): you can sell
    clotted cream even in tins
  medicines
  aircraft, motor or cycle accessories
  tobacco and cigarettes

newspapers
books at railway terminals
passport photographs

The local authority may allow opening up to 10 a.m. on Sunday for the sale of bread, fish and groceries, and in holiday resorts may suspend all the restrictions for up to 18 Sundays in any year. Market stalls count as shops but certain markets, e.g. Petticoat Lane, have been granted the right to open on Sundays. Jewish shopkeepers can open to 2 p.m. on Sunday but must close all day Saturday.

In reality the Sunday opening hours are flouted regularly and many local authorities do nothing about enforcing them. The confused state of the law only makes matters worse, as many people do not know which shopkeepers are acting legally and which are not. So if you go into a chemist on a Sunday you cannot buy a film but you can buy medicines: films can only be bought at museums, zoos, public gardens or galleries!

Key points

- Is there a contract?
- Which contract terms apply?
- What are those terms?
- What duties do you owe apart from under a contract?

5

Crimes against consumers

Outline

This chapter summarizes your obligations to consumers, focusing in particular on:

- weights and measures
- trade descriptions
- misleading prices
- food and drugs

Weights and Measures Act 1985

The 1985 Act and numerous detailed regulations lay down rules to be observed by businesses. If you need to know about them you should contact your local weights and measures department which is part of the county or borough council.

Local weights and measures departments have inspectors who inspect weights and measures to make sure customers are not being cheated. Breaches of the Acts or regulations can give rise to prosecution which can be started either by the local weights and measures authority or the crown prosecution service.

Consumer Protection Act 1987

In addition to the civil obligations imposed by this Act (see chapter 4), it also imposes criminal sanctions. It is a criminal offence to supply any *consumer* goods which fail to comply with the general safety requirement. Prosecutions are made by the Trading Standards

Officer. The maximum fine is now £2000 or a maximum prison sentence of six months or both!

Under the same Act the Secretary of State can make safety regulations so as to secure that goods are safe. Such safety regulations can extend to

- the content, design, packaging or construction of goods;
- the banning of certain goods.

Orders have been made in respect of furniture and fire hazards, three-wheeled terrain motor vehicles, babies' dummies and many other items. The Act gives trading standards officers power to search premises and seize goods.

Misleading prices and sales labels

The Consumer Protection Act 1987 controls the giving of misleading prices for any goods, services or facilities to consumers. Unlike the Trade Descriptions Acts (see later in this chapter) which apply to business and consumer sales, the misleading prices legislation only applies to consumers.

What is a misleading price? The Act lays down certain rules and is backed up by the Consumer Protection (Code of Practice of Traders on Price Indications) Approval Order 1988.

Price comparisons

1 Terms such as 'normal price', 'usual price', etc. should make it clear whose price is referred to, e.g. 'our normal price'.
2 In a price comparison the previous price should be the last price at which the product was available to the consumer in the previous six months.
3 The product should have been available to consumers at that price for at least 28 consecutive days in the previous six months. (NB this does not apply to food and drink or non-food perishables with a shelf life of less than six weeks.)
4 The previous price should have applied in the same shop where the reduced price is now being offered.

5 The higher price and the offer price must be given. This need not be adhered to if the comparison is clear and positive, e.g. 'Sale Price £3 – Previous Price £10 from 10 to 31 December'.

Comparisons are allowed with recommended retail prices. Here is a brief guide to some standard pricing forms:

Reduced: £15	Illegal ⎫	Not enough comparative
~~*£15*~~ *: £10*	Illegal ⎭	information given
Last months price: £25	Illegal	Should specify 'our last
Now: *£10*		month's price' and that price must have been available for at least 28 consecutive days in that store
Sale Price: £25	Illegal	
Recommended Retail Price: £10	Legal	So long as it is a genuine
Our Price: *£8*		retail price
Recommended Price £10	Illegal	Must specify *Retail* Price,
Our Price: *£8*		'RRP' or 'Man. Rec. Price' will pass

Breach of the Act can result in a £2000 maximum fine in the Crown Court or a fine at the discretion of a magistrate in the magistrate's courts.

The trader can argue the follow defences:

- that he took all reasonable steps and exercised all due diligence to avoid committing the offence; and
- that the offence was due to the default of another (just as under the Trade Descriptions Act, see later in this chapter); or
- that the offence was due to reliance on information given by another provided it was reasonable for him to do so.

Trade Descriptions Acts 1968 and 1972

The Trade Descriptions Acts make it a criminal offence to make false descriptions about goods or services, e.g. 'Made in France' when manufactured in Taiwan. To sell such goods is also a breach of contract if it is a term of the contract, but in this section we are concerned with criminal law only.

This should be a simple area of law easily understood by trader and consumer alike but unfortunately a series of court cases funded by large retail operations have made the law very complex and weak. The legislation is enforced by the trading standards department who are a part of the local authority. Private prosecutions can be mounted but are rare. The maximum penalty on conviction in the magistrates court is £2000 and in the Crown Court a maximum term of imprisonment of two years or an unlimited fine. There are different rules for goods and services.

Goods

The following characteristics of goods must be accurately described:

- Quantity, size or gauge, e.g. selling moisturizing cream in jars with false bottoms is a criminal offence if the customer is led to believe more is being purchased than is really being sold.
- Method of manufacture, production or processing, e.g. 'hand made'.
- Composition, e.g. the court held in one case that it was a breach to advertise that an item of furniture was ready assembled when it was not.
- Fitness for purpose, strength and performance, e.g. 'beautiful car', 'immaculate condition', 'mechanically superb'.
- Testing, e.g. 'tested by *Which?*'
- Approved by any person, e.g. 'approved by Oxford University' or 'to BSI standards'.
- Person by whom goods manufactured, e.g. putting Bass beer in some other brewer's bottles would be a breach.
- Other history, e.g. it is misleading to describe a car as having had one owner when it has had five.

There are two defences to a prosecution:

1 That the offence was someone else's fault
2 That it was not realized the description was false

To successfully argue that the offence was someone else's fault the defendant must show

- that it was due to a mistake or the result of false information given to him, or
- that it was due to the default of some other person,

and

- that he took all reasonable precautions to avoid the offence.

In one case Tesco managed to avoid liability for putting up erroneous 'special offer' signs by blaming their shop manger whose responsibility it was to check such matters. The false description was thus 'due to the default of another'. Not all employers will be willing to shift the blame on to a named employee who had specific responsibility for the breach of the Act, but it is certainly possible!

If a court finds a limited company guilty of an offence under the Act it can also find a director, manager or secretary or other similar officer guilty if the offence has been made 'with the consent and connivance of, or found to be attributable to any neglect of' that person. So the protection of limited liability can be lifted.

Services

The laws on falsely describing services are weaker than those on falsely describing goods.

It is a criminal offence for a trader

- to make a statement which he knows to be false; or
- recklessly to make a false statement (e.g. he did not bother to check the truth of his statement) as in *Wings* v. *Ellis*.

The case of *Wings* v. *Ellis* concerned a hotel brochure advertising air conditioned rooms, but in fact there was no air conditioning. The company was found to have committed a criminal offence by wrongly describing the rooms.

Food and drugs legislation

The Food Act 1984 and the myriad regulations made under it regulate the production, distribution and sale of food. The

81

environmental health officer, who is an employee of the local authority, is the official charged with supervising compliance with the Act. If you need to know anything about the legislation you should consult him or a solicitor.

Breach of the Food Acts can give rise to criminal liabilities. Just as under the Trade Descriptions Act, directors and other officers can be found guilty as well as the limited companies for which they work. If found guilty the maximum fine is £2000 in the magistrates court; in the Crown Court an offender can be sentenced to a maximum of two years imprisonment or a fine or both.

Key points

- Directors can be made liable for breaches of the criminal law by limited companies.
- Fines and/or imprisonment can be imposed.

6

Employment matters

Outline

This chapter considers your obligations to your employees including:

- hiring staff
- employment contracts
- unfair dismissal
- redundancy

Employment law is restrictive. You cannot just 'hire and fire' staff. There is a very good series of pamphlets available free of charge from the Department of Employment or the Advisory and Conciliation Service (ACAS) on many of the subjects covered here – these will give greater details (see appendix 1).

Adverts and job interviews

Job advertisements and interviews have to comply with the Sex Discrimination Act and the Race Relations Act. This is a complex field where you can easily breach the law by indirect discrimination.

Sex discrimination

You cannot treat a person less favourably because of his/her sex or marital status. Hence all these are unlawful job adverts:

'Male Traffic Warden', 'Female Driver', 'Married Man', 'Single Men Only'

There are certain exceptions:

1 When required by Act of Parliament: the NCB can advertise for 'male coal miners' as women are not allowed to work in underground mines.
2 When sex is a genuine occupational qualification, e.g. 'female lavatory attendant'.
3 Jobs in private households: if the job involves a degree of intimate or physical contact, e.g. you can advertise for a live-in female companion but not a male gardener.
4 Employment outside Great Britain: 'male teacher needed to work in Saudi Arabia' is legal.

Make sure your interviews are not discriminatory, e.g. don't say 'we only employ women as tea ladies'.

Racial Discrimination

It is unlawful to treat any person less favourably on the grounds of race (i.e. colour, race, nationality, citizenship or ethnic or national origin). Hence it is unlawful to advertise in a discriminatory manner: none of these would be legal:

'Englishman required to manage Club', 'British passport holders only'

But there are exceptions:

1 Genuine occupational needs, e.g. an Indian waiter in an Indian restaurant.
2 Employment outside Great Britain, e.g. 'Black teacher for position in Nigeria'.

Breach

Any breach of the Act allows a complainant to make an application to an industrial tribunal to claim compensation. An application has to be made within three months of the breach of the Act. The maximum compensation that can be awarded for a breach of either the Sex Discrimination or the Race Relation Acts is £8925.

Criminal records

Potential employers also need to know their rights about potential employees' criminal records. Under the Rehabilitation of Offenders Act certain convictions become 'spent' after a certain time, as shown in exhibit 1.

Exhibit 1

Sentence	Rehabilitation period from date of conviction
Prison: 2½ years or more	Never
Prison: over 6 months but less than 2½ years	10 years
Prison: not more than 6 months	7 years
Fine	5 years
Conditional discharge: binding over	1 year
Probation order	1 year
Borstal	7 years
Absolute discharge	6 months

'Spent' convictions do not normally have to be disclosed when applying for a job, except in certain cases if the applicant is asked; these include: prison staff, teachers, doctors, dentists, barristers, solicitors, vets and other professionals. A person with an 'unspent' conviction, who fails to disclose this when asked, could be fairly dismissed subsequently if the conviction was discovered.

Disabled staff

Employers with more than 20 staff have to see that their workforce is comprised of at least 3 per cent registered disabled persons. Under the Act an employer should not fill any vacancy that arises with an able-bodied employee unless at that date the employer already employs his quota of registered disabled people.

Offering a job

Once you have selected a potential employee, what then? Do you have to draw up a written contract? Answer: 'no'. But just because you have not made a formal written offer does not mean there is no contract. Employment contracts can be oral. The law will enforce the terms of the contract and if nothing is written down then in the event of a dispute the courts or an industrial tribunal will work out what the parties intended.

Contracts of employment

Employee or self-employed?

You have to be able to distinguish whether a person is an employee or self-employed. The reason being that each status has different legal implications. This chapter deal only with employees. The distinction between an employee and a self-employed person (also known as an 'independent contractor') is at times very subtle. The principal differences between an employee and a self-employed person are

1 a self-employed person controls his or her own hours and method of work;
2 a self-employed person need not give nor be given any notice to end the contract, unless the contract says otherwise;
3 a self-employed person will, over a period of time, normally work for a number of different organizations;
4 self-employed persons do not pay PAYE and pay all their NI themselves. There is no employer's NI contribution;
5 self-employed persons are ineligible for unemployment benefit, statutory sick pay, compensation for unfair dismissal, redundancy payments or holiday pay.

Written statement of employment

Although you do not have to draw up a formal employment contract the law requires that the employer gives the employee a written statement of the main terms of the employment contract within thirteen weeks of the employee starting work. It is sensible to issue this as soon as the employee is recruited. The written particulars must state the following.

Names The names of both employer and employee must be given. Fairly obvious, but if there are a number of companies within a group make sure the right company's name is down.

Date The date when the employment started. You also have to state whether or not this employment is continuous with any previous service. This is important in connection with notice, compensation for unfair dismissal and redundancy payments where length of service determines the employee's rights.

Pay The rate of pay: is it payable weekly or monthly? Are there any bonus payments?

Job title It is best to make this as general as possible so as to give maximum flexibility to move employees around as circumstances change, without running the risk of the employee claiming that you have changed the terms of the contract.

Holiday entitlement What are the holidays? Are they paid? Do certain days have to be taken at set times, e.g. August or Christmas? Do you expect the employee to work on bank holidays? If so, say so, for otherwise you will not be able to enforce this.

Pensions Is there a pension scheme? What are the employer's and the employee's contributions? What are the details of the scheme?

Sickness and injury What are the firm's rules about sickness? Is sick pay paid? If so, for how long? Is the statutory sick pay scheme operated?

Notice What notice must be given to terminate the contract? The minimum period of notice must be set out which cannot be less than the minimum laid down by statute (see exhibit 2). Note that these rules apply to *employers*. They do *not* apply to employees. An employee only has to give one weeks notice if he or she has been employed for four weeks or more, *unless* the contract of employment requires more notice. Hence, it is very important to stipulate in the written particulars an appropriate notice period for the employee to give.

Exhibit 2

Length of employment	Length of notice by employer
Under 1 month	Nil
1 month to 2 years	1 week
2 years to 12 years	1 week for each full year of employment
Over 12 years	12 weeks

Hours of Work   What is the normal working week? Note that an employee does not have to work overtime unless his contract says so.

Discipline at Work   What are the disciplinary procedures? What is the mechanism for an employee who wishes to appeal against being disciplined? This does not apply if there are less than 20 employees in the service of the employer, together, if relevant, with any associated employer.

Complaints   To whom should the employee make a complaint?

No written particulars

If you do not supply written particulars the employee can complain to an industrial tribunal and the tribunal can order you to hand over written particulars, but there is no other formal sanction on an employer who fails to issue them.

Other details to be notified to employees

The Industrial Relations Code of Practice issued by ACAS sets out the behaviour to be expected of a 'reasonable' employer. It is not an offence to ignore the Code, but an employer who disregards its provisions may find that an industrial tribunal will not be favourably disposed towards him.

Specific requirements

Although you have only to issue the written particulars, it is wise to go beyond that and deal not only with the matters dealt with in the

Code of Practice (see above) but also other matters which are of a special relevance in each particular case:

1 Job mobility: will the employee be expected to move home if the employer wants him to work elsewhere?
2 Non-competition: does the employer want to limit the freedom of the employee to work for competitors or customers? Does he want to restrain the employee from soliciting customers after the end of the contract?
3 Is the employee's pay suspended during layoffs, e.g. because of bad weather or industrial action? The common law rule is that the employee is entitled to be paid while laid off.

Employee's duties and employer's rights

Employee's duties – reasonable care

The employee must take reasonable care in doing his job. He must not be negligent. If he is, the employer can sue him for the loss he suffers because of the employee's negligence. Surprisingly few such cases come to the courts, mainly no doubt because the risk is insured against or the employers do not want the adverse publicity. Anyway, most employees are not worth suing – they may not have the money to pay any damages awarded! But in one case a bank sued a branch manager for negligently sanctioning a loan. The branch manager was ordered to pay £36,000 damages.

Employee's duties – obey lawful orders

An employee must only obey lawful orders. He can refuse to use unsafe machines or fiddle the VAT return. He can also refuse to carry out work not within the terms of his contract of employment: hence the need to have a widely drafted job specification.

Employer's rights – discipline

The employer has the right to discipline his staff.

The ultimate sanction that an employer has for dealing with an employee's breach of contract is to end the contract and dismiss the employee (see later in this chapter). But the employer can discipline the employee as well. ACAS has published a Code of Practice on disciplinary rules and disciplinary procedures. This disciplinary Code sets out the behaviour to be expected of a reasonable employer. A copy of it can be obtained from ACAS.

The recommended procedure for handling a minor breach of contract is

- formal oral warning or, for a more serious offence, a written warning;
- further misconduct may warrant a final written warning;
- further misconduct may lead to dismissal;

The written warnings should set out the offence and the likely consequences if it is repeated.

As part of the disciplinary procedure an employer might take the following actions.

Suspend an employee on full pay This is not a breach of contract by the employer. Although this is another 'grey area' the general view is that an employee has no legal remedy if he is given no work. The employer's obligation is to pay him but not to give the employee work – this may not apply to skilled workers who need to practise their skill.

Suspend an employee without pay Unless this is specifically provided for in the employment contract this is a breach of contract. Should you include this?

Fines or deductions These have to be authorized by the contract and are subject to the Wages Act 1986 (see next section).

Transfer to another location Unless the employment contract gives the employer the right to move employees, this is a breach of contract.

Employee's rights

Itemized pay statements

Employers must provide their staff with itemized pay statements specifying

- the gross pay;
- the net pay;
- any deductions from the gross pay, stating how much the deduction is and why it has been made.

Beware: if the employer breaks this law the employee can apply to an industrial tribunal at any time during his employment or within three months after the end of the employment. If unnotified deductions have been made, the tribunal can order the employer to pay a sum to the employee equal to the unnotified deductions made during the thirteen weeks before the date of the application to the tribunal. So an employer can be ordered to pay to the employee the amount of NI, pension or tax deductions even though the employer was entitled to make those deductions, just because he failed to notify the employee!

Employee's rights – deductions from wages

Under the Wages Act 1986 no deductions from wages can be made unless

- it is required by statute (e.g. PAYE); or
- it is authorized by the contract; or
- the worker has given written consent.

However, an employer can deduct from wages

- any overpayments for wages or expenses;
- any deduction as a result of disciplinary proceedings;
- any deduction ordered by a court, e.g. an attachment of earnings order.

Note: in retail trades no deductions can be made even if sanctioned by the contract for cash shortages or stock deficiencies which exceed 10 per cent of the worker's gross pay.

If there is a breach of these provisions, the employee can complain to an industrial tribunal within three months.

Employees' rights – minimum wages

There are about 50 wage councils established in industries where trade union activity is low and employees can easily be exploited.

The wage councils have the powers to lay down minimum terms and conditions and especially concern themselves with setting minimum rates of pay and holiday entitlement. Some 3½ million workers are subject to the jurisdiction of the wage councils and these include

- hairdressing;
- clothing trades;
- laundries (excluding dry cleaners and launderettes).

The wages inspectorate at the Department of Employment is responsible for enforcing wage councils' orders (see appendix 2). They can provide a full list of trades covered by the wage councils and have the power to prosecute employers who pay less than the minimum rates. In reality there are so few wage inspectors that they only prosecute in the worst cases. The employee has the right to sue the employer for up to six years underpaid wages.

Equal pay for men and women

The Equal Pay Act 1970 requires equal pay for 'like work' regardless of the employee's sex. The law implies into each contract of employment a clause known as an 'equality clause'. An employee can apply to an industrial tribunal at any time during the employment or within six months of leaving the job and claim damages. The tribunal can award damages including pay due to the employee if he or she has been paid less than a man or woman in a comparable job. No more than two years arrears can be awarded.

The equal pay laws are extremely complicated and if an employee raises an equal pay issue, an employer is well advised to take specialist legal advice.

Statutory sick pay ('SSP')

If an employee is off sick for more than four days in a row including Saturdays and Sundays, he or she may be able to get SSP. In the New Employers Starter Pack available from the DSS and Inland Revenue (ref. P4) is an excellent simple guide (see chapter 8). If you have problems ring the Social Security Advice Line for Employers (0800 393539) – the phone call is free.

Maternity – ante-natal care

All pregnant women can have a reasonable amount of time off work on full pay so as to receive ante-natal care. This applies to all appointments and to all employees, even to part-timers.

Statutory maternity pay ('SMP')

To qualify for SMP a woman must

- be employed full-time, i.e. work more than 16 hours per week;
- have been employed by her employer for at least two years (by the beginning of the eleventh week before her baby is due);
- continue in employment until at least eleven weeks prior to the expected date of birth; if she is off sick at the eleventh week she will have 'continued in employment' as she will still be employed at that date, albeit that she is off work, sick;
- she must tell her employer that she intends to stop work because she is pregnant at least three weeks before she is due to leave (this does *not* have to be written notice).

What is SMP? SMP is six weeks wages at 90 per cent of the woman's normal weekly wage, minus the DSS maternity allowance. It should be paid either in a lump sum when the woman ceases to work or on a weekly or monthly basis. It is paid net of tax and NI contributions. If it is not, the employee can complain to the Department of Social Security within three months of the date when the last payment was due.

The employer can set off the SMP he has paid plus 7½ per cent against his National Insurance contributions. If the sum paid is greater than the employer's NI contributions in that month he can claim a refund from the DSS.

Maternity – a woman's right to return to work

A woman who has left to give birth can claim her job back after the birth if she complies with the following conditions:

- She has been employed full-time and continuously employed (see last section).
- She must notify her employer in writing at least three weeks

before she leaves that she intends to stop work because of her pregnancy and wants to return to work after the birth – the letter must state her expected date of confinement/delivery.

- Once seven weeks have elapsed after the expected date of birth, the employer can ask her to give written confirmation that she intends to return to work. He must warn her of the consequences of not replying in the set time. If she does not reply within two weeks of his letter, she loses her right to return to work.
- She must return to work within 29 weeks of the birth.
- She must give at least three weeks written notice before she returns to work. Note: different rules apply to firms with less than six employees (including the returning mother) at the time she left. If it is not 'reasonably practicable' to give her her old job back or another suitable job the employer does not have to re-employ her.
- Redundancy and unfair dismissal rights accrue during the period of absence.
- On returning, the employee must be paid and have the same terms and conditions as before, but this does not mean that, unless her contract of employment was very specific, she can claim her old job back. The employer has to offer a suitable alternative job. If he does not she could claim unfair dismissal.

Time off for public duties

An employee can take time off work to carry out his or her duties as

- magistrate;
- local councillor;
- member of a tribunal;
- regional or area health authority worker.

Note: the time off is unpaid. This applies to all employees, even if they have worked for less than two years.

- This does not apply to part-timers
- The amount of time allowed must be 'reasonable' (see chapter 5)

Time off for trade union activities

Trade union officials (not members) can take a 'reasonable' amount of *paid* time off work for

- industrial relations duties between employers and employees (e.g. wage negotiations) and
- industrial relations training on courses approved by the union or the TUC.

Union members can take a 'reasonable' amount of unpaid time off work to carry out their trade union activities.

What is a 'reasonable' amount of time? The ACAS Code of Practice on this gives no definition: clearly it will depend on the employee's position, the pressures on the business, the size of the firm, etc.

If an employee is refused time off either for union duties or activities, he can complain within three months to an industrial tribunal which has the power to award compensation assessed not only on the loss incurred but also taking into account any insult or injury to him. These rights apply to any full-time employee; the employee does *not* need to have worked for two years to qualify.

Working hours

There is no set maximum hours for work for men either per day or per week, which is surprising in this era of sexual equality given that there is legislation limiting the hours that children or women can work. The Health and Safety Executive are responsible for supervising the law – if you want further details, check with them (see appendix 2).

Paid holidays

An employee is entitled to have public holidays off, unless his contract requires him to work on these days. If the contract does not state anything about paid holiday, a court will infer a right to a reasonable amount of paid holiday, taking into account the custom and practice in the industry.

Safety

The Health and Safety at Work etc. Act 1974 obliges employers to ensure, so far as reasonably practicable, the health, safety and welfare of all their employees. This means

- plant and systems of work have to be safe and without risk to health;
- employers must make arrangements to ensure safety and absence of risks to health;
- providing information, instruction, training and supervision to staff;
- providing a working environment that is safe;
- drawing up a health and safety policy statement if you have five or more employees and bringing it to their notice;
- providing, free, any protective clothing or equipment required by law.

Moreover, the courts have established over the years that employers must

- employ competent staff;
- provide adequate materials.

In addition to the Health and Safety at Work etc. Act, particular statutes cover various industries. The employer may need to be aware of the Factories Acts, the Office, Shops and Railway Premises Act, the Mines and Quarries Act, etc. The Factories Acts are the most important, covering laundries and dry cleaners, garages, potteries, brickworks, construction sites, docks and warehouses as well as factories.

If an employee is injured because of a breach of the Factories Acts the employer is liable, even if he has not been negligent. Further details of which pieces of legislation apply to a particular industry can be found by contacting the Health and Safety Executive.

Dismissal

Termination notice

Generally you can only end a contract by giving proper notice as laid down by statute (see earlier in this chapter) or by the contract. Unless the contract says otherwise, oral notice will do.

If an employee has been guilty of gross misconduct, e.g. theft at work, major or serious breaches of discipline or assaults on staff, this justifies immediate or 'summary' dismissal, without notice. Employers need to be very careful about dismissing without notice because this could cause problems about unfair dismissal (see later in this chapter).

Wrongful dismissal

If the employer terminates the contract without notice and with no justification, what can the employee do? Answer: bring a claim for *wrongful* dismissal in the county court or High Court (if the claim is for more than £5000). The amount claimed will be salary due during the notice period. However, as the employee is expected to take 'reasonable' steps to 'mitigate' or reduce his loss, the employer can argue he should have found an alternative job. If the employer can convince the court that the employee has failed to mitigate his loss then the court may award reduced or no damages. If the employee finds another job at a similar or higher salary he has suffered no loss and can claim nothing. If the court does award damages it will reduce the gross sum due by the PAYE and NI that should have been deducted and the amount of any unemployment benefit received.

No notice from the employee

If the employee gives no notice, what can the employer do? Answer: sue the employee for breach of contract and seek damages for any losses sustained by the employer during the notice period as a result of the breach. The employee will argue that it should have been possible to find a replacement. But if that argument can be overcome (e.g. because the employee had unusual skills or no replacement was available) the employer could recover damages, e.g. for loss of a major order. In fact such cases are very rare, both because the chances of actually recovering any damages awarded may be slim and the courts are not very sympathetic to such claims.

Salary in lieu

Can an employer pay salary in lieu of notice? Answer: 'yes'. As an employer does not normally have to provide work for his employees he need not let an employee work out his notice. Provided he pays him for his notice period he has complied with the contract.

Reasons for dismissal

Can a dismissed employee ask for the reasons? Answer: 'yes'. An employer must give written reasons for the dismissal within 14 days of the request, but only if the employee asks. The reasons given must be sufficiently detailed to show why the employee was dismissed. If written reasons are not given within 14 days, the employee can apply to an industrial tribunal. The tribunal can order the employer to pay three weeks wages for failing to give written reasons.

References

An employer does not have to give a reference for his previous employees. If he does give one he owes a duty both to the former employee and the prospective employer to ensure that the reference is accurate. If he gives a glowing reference for an incompetent employee in the hope of seeing the back of him, he could be sued by the new employer if he suffers loss as a result of the employee's activities. The person giving the reference can write a disclaimer, e.g. 'This reference is given without liability'. This may not be effective because of the Unfair Contract Terms Act 1977 – a court might rule that it is not 'reasonable' (see chapter 4).

Beware too of the Servant's Characters Act 1792; if an employer makes 'a false and fraudulent' statement about an employee's character, he can be prosecuted in a magistrates court! You have been warned.

Fixed-term contracts

A fixed-term contract is for an agreed period, e.g. one year or six months. No notice is needed to terminate the contract; in a glorious phrase much beloved by lawyers 'it expires by the effluxion of time'. In other words, when the time's up, that's an end of it.

Unfair dismissal

Most employers are very worried about the unfair dismissal legislation and seem to think it allows employees jobs for life, and that breach results in massive fines. Neither is true. In 1986–7 only 33.7 per cent of applications for unfair dismissal were successful and the average award was £1805.

Qualifying conditions

An employee is within the unfair dismissal legislation only if

- he is full-time (i.e. works more than 16 hours a week);
- he has worked continuously for two years (part-timers who work at least eight hours a week qualify after five years continuous employment).

The crucial test is the two-year period; therefore many employers review staff just before the two years are up. The employees' notice period counts towards the two years. The legislation does not apply to persons who have reached the normal retirement age for that category of employees. Note: There is no qualifying period if an employee claims to have been dismissed because of sex, race, married status or because of trade union activities.

Beware: if you agree with an employee who is covered by the Unfair Dismissal legislation the terms of the termination of his contract, that agreement is not binding on the employee unless it has been sanctioned by ACAS and Form COT3 has been completed. This means that unless that form is signed the employee can take the agreed settlement moneys and still claim unfair dismissal!

Was the employee dismissed?

This sounds fairly stupid. It is surely obvious whether or not an employee has been dismissed, but in reality matters are not always totally straightforward. A dismissal occurs not just when an employee is sacked. An employee can claim unfair dismissal

- if it is a constructive dismissal (see next section);
- if a fixed period contract comes to an end (see later in this chapter).

Constructive dismissal

As the name implies this is when an employee resigns but claims he has been forced into resignation by the employer's breach of contract.

For an employee to establish he has been constructively dismissed he must show that the employer has broken the employment contract in a serious way. A minor breach will not do. Examples include

- unilaterally reducing pay;
- unilaterally changing duties;
- insisting on the employee working hours that are not covered by the contract;
- insisting on transferring an employee beyond a reasonable travelling distance.

Note: these will *not* constitute a breach of contract if the contract authorizes them (see earlier in this chapter).

The employer also has an implied duty not to undermine the trust and confidence in the employment relationship. Breach of this can cause a constructive dismissal, e.g. *Courtaulds Northern Textiles Ltd.* v. *Andrew*. Mr Andrew had worked for 18 years good service. He was told 'you can't do the bloody job anyway'. He left and successfully claimed constructive dismissal.

Expiry of a fixed-term contract

An employee with a fixed-term contract may be able to claim he has been 'dismissed' if it is not renewed when it expires and he has two years continuous service. But the employer can get round this in a contract for a year or more by inserting a clause stating that non-renewal will not be unfair dismissal.

Was the dismissal 'fair'?

All dismissals are deemed to be unfair. The burden of proof is on the employer to show that the dismissal is 'fair'. The potentially fair reasons for dismissal are as follows.

The employee is incapable, incompetent or lacks qualifications

The employer should make a proper appraisal of the employee's performance, warn him and give an opportunity to improve. In cases involving high degrees of professional skill where one lapse could be disastrous, one instance of incompetence will justify immediate dismissal, without the need to give warnings, etc.

How much time do you have to give people to get their act together? There is no set rule – it must be a 'reasonable' period. If after the trial period the employee has not improved, then the employer will be able to claim that a dismissal is fair.

Cases of ill health present complex issues. An employer cannot just sack sick employees; he is expected to give them reasonable job security. Employees who are on sick leave for a long time, e.g. with a slipped disc, can only be fairly dismissed if the employer acts reasonably, namely

- finds out as much as possible about the employee's condition and obtains full information including medical reports;
- gives the employee a written warning;
- uses every effort to find alternative work for the employee.

Misconduct

Refusing to obey lawful orders What is or is not a lawful order depends in part on the terms of the employment contract. Is a waiter expected to wash up the dishes? What if he refuses to do so? If his contract defines his job as 'waiter' he could refuse to wash the dishes. If he was dismissed this would be 'unfair'. Back to the written conditions of employment!

Breach of discipline For example fighting, swearing, theft, drunkenness, falsifying time sheets and lateness would be considered to be a breach of discipline. An employer may want to cover more particular rules of conduct, e.g. no smoking. If so he should cover them in the written particulars.

Criminal offences committed away from work Not all criminal offences committed away from work will justify dismissal. They must in some way affect the business or in some way undermine the confidence which the employer has in his own employees, e.g. dishonesty.

Breach of the law

It is not unfair to dismiss an employee whose employment would be a breach of the law, e.g. a driver who had lost his driving licence.

Some other substantial reason

This is the 'sweeper' or long-stop of the unfair dismissal legislation. An employer can justify a dismissal if it is for 'some other substantial reason'. What does this mean? Important cases have involved the following.

union agreement	dismissal for refusing to abide by an agreement negotiated with a union was fair
sexual orientation of the employee	dismissal of a homosexual handyman at a children's home after he was involved in a homosexual incident, not involving children, was fair
personality differences	dismissal of a woman who taunted her male colleague about her sexual relationship with a boy almost half her age was fair

Did the employer act reasonably?

Even if an employer has a fair reason for dismissal, if he acts unreasonably that will convert a 'fair' dismissal into an unfair one.

He must act reasonably throughout the dismissal procedure and must make sure he abides by his own disciplinary code and gives adequate warning.

Breach of the employer's own procedures or the ACAS Code of Practice (see earlier in this chapter) will probably make a fair dismissal unfair. In three cases a dismissal is automatically unfair. They are

- dismissal because of a 'spent' conviction under the Rehabilitation of Offenders Act 1974 (see earlier in this chapter);
- dismissal for trade union membership or activity or non-membership;
- dismissal for pregnancy or a reason connected with pregnancy.

Note: employees dismissed for trade union membership or non-membership do *not* have to have two years continuous employment and the age restrictions do not apply to them.

Compensation for unfair dismissal

Despite popular myth, industrial tribunal awards are, on average, small. But the tribunal need not award money. It can order an employer to comply with the following.

1 Reinstate the employee in his or her old job. Because of the personality issues involved, reinstatement orders are very rare.
2 Re-employ the employee in a different job. Again, very unusual.

In fact 98.9 per cent of awards are in cash. The award is divided into two:

1 the basic award (up to £5520)
2 the compensatory award (up to £8925)

These are 1990 figures. The limits are reviewed as at 1 April in each year.

The basic award

The basic award gives the employee the same amount of money as he would have got if he was made redundant and was paid statutory redundancy. The payment is based on

- age,
- length of service,
- weekly pay but subject to a maximum of £184. 2io

See exhibit 3 which gives a ready reckoner for working out the award.

Exhibit 3 Compensation for unfair dismissal: how many weeks' wages?

Age (years)	2	3	4	5	6	7	8	9	10	11	12	13	14	15	16	17	18	19	20
20	1	1	1	1															
21	1	1½	1½	1½	1½														
22	1	1½	2	2	2	2													
23	1½	2	2½	3	3	3	3												
24	2	2½	3	3½	4	4	4	4											
25	2	3	3½	4	4½	5	5	5	5										
26	2	3	4	4½	5	5½	6	6	6	6									
27	2	3	4	5	5½	6	6½	7	7	7	7								
28	2	3	4	5	6	6½	7	7½	8	8	8	8							
29	2	3	4	5	6	7	7½	8	8½	9	9	9	9						
30	2	3	4	5	6	7	8	8½	9	9½	10	10	10	10					
31	2	3	4	5	6	7	8	9	9½	10	10½	11	11	11	11				
32	2	3	4	5	6	7	8	9	10	10½	11	11½	12	12	12	12			
33	2	3	4	5	6	7	8	9	10	11	11½	12	12½	13	13	13	13		
34	2	3	4	5	6	7	8	9	10	11	12	12½	13	13½	14	14	14	14	
35	2	3	4	5	6	7	8	9	10	11	12	13	13½	14	14½	15	15	15	15
36	2	3	4	5	6	7	8	9	10	11	12	13	14	14½	15	15½	16	16	16
37	2	3	4	5	6	7	8	9	10	11	12	13	14	15	15½	16	16½	17	17
38	2	3	4	5	6	7	8	9	10	11	12	13	14	15	16	16½	17	17½	18
39	2	3	4	5	6	7	8	9	10	11	12	13	14	15	16	17	17½	18	18½
40	2	3	4	5	6	7	8	9	10	11	12	13	14	15	16	17	18	18½	19
41	2	3	4	5	6	7	8	9	10	11	12	13	14	15	16	17	18	19	19½
42	2½	3½	4½	5½	6½	7½	8½	9½	10½	11½	12½	13½	14½	15½	16½	17½	18½	19½	20½
43	3	4	5	6	7	8	9	10	11	12	13	14	15	16	17	18	19	20	21
44	3	4½	5½	6½	7½	8½	9½	10½	11½	12½	13½	14½	15½	16½	17½	18½	19½	20½	21½
45	3	4½	6	7	8	9	10	11	12	13	14	15	16	17	18	19	20	21	22
46	3	4½	6	7½	8½	9½	10½	11½	12½	13½	14½	15½	16½	17½	18½	19½	20½	21½	22½
47	3	4½	6	7½	9	10	11	12	13	14	15	16	17	18	19	20	21	22	23
48	3	4½	6	7½	9	10½	11½	12½	13½	14½	15½	16½	17½	18½	19½	20½	21½	22½	23½
49	3	4½	6	7½	9	10½	12	13	14	15	16	17	18	19	20	21	22	23	24
50	3	4½	6	7½	9	10½	12	13½	14½	15½	16½	17½	18½	19½	20½	21½	22½	23½	24½
51	3	4½	6	7½	9	10½	12	13½	15	16	17	18	19	20	21	22	23	24	25
52	3	4½	6	7½	9	10½	12	13½	15	16½	17½	18½	19½	20½	21½	22½	23½	24½	25½
53	3	4½	6	7½	9	10½	12	13½	15	16½	18	19	20	21	22	23	24	25	26
54	3	4½	6	7½	9	10½	12	13½	15	16½	18	19½	20½	21½	22½	23½	24½	25½	26½
55	3	4½	6	7½	9	10½	12	13½	15	16½	18	19½	21	22	23	24	25	26	27
56	3	4½	6	7½	9	10½	12	13½	15	16½	18	19½	21	22½	23½	24½	25½	26½	27½
57	3	4½	6	7½	9	10½	12	13½	15	16½	18	19½	21	22½	24	25	26	27	28
58	3	4½	6	7½	9	10½	12	13½	15	16½	18	19½	21	22½	24	25½	26½	27½	28½
59	3	4½	6	7½	9	10½	12	13½	15	16½	18	19½	21	22½	24	25½	27	28	29
60	3	4½	6	7½	9	10½	12	13½	15	16½	18	19½	21	22½	24	25½	27	28½	29½
61	3	4½	6	7½	9	10½	12	13½	15	16½	18	19½	21	22½	24	25½	27	28½	30
62	3	4½	6	7½	9	10½	12	13½	15	16½	18	19½	21	22½	24	25½	27	28½	30
63	3	4½	6	7½	9	10½	12	13½	15	16½	18	19½	21	22½	24	25½	27	28½	30
64	3	4½	6	7½	9	10½	12	13½	15	16½	18	19½	21	22½	24	25½	27	28½	30

Men only (rows 60–64)

The tribunal can reduce the basic award if

- the employee's conduct makes it just and equitable to do so;
- the employee has unreasonably refused an offer of reinstatement.

Note: if the employee is within one year of the state retirement age, he/she will lose one-twelfth of his/her compensation for each whole month after his/her birthday, e.g. a man aged 64½ will lose half his award; if he was aged 64 years and 1 month he would lose one-twelfth.

Calculating the compensatory award

The compensatory award is intended to compensate the employee for the financial loss suffered by him because of his dismissal. The award can cover the following losses.

Lost earnings up to the date of the industrial tribunal hearing   That is money that should have been paid during the notice period. This could also be recovered by an action in the county court or High Court for wrongful dismissal (see earlier in this chapter). Hence there is no need for the employee to bring both a court action for wrongful dismissal and an industrial tribunal action for unfair dismissal.

The employee is under an obligation to reduce or 'mitigate' his loss (see earlier in this chapter). If he has not done this, the compensatory award may be reduced.

Future loss of earnings   The employee has to prove potential future loss. Tribunals are reluctant to extrapolate losses forward more than five years. If the employee is still out of work at the date of the hearing, then he will have a continuing loss and the tribunal can make an award based on that. If he is in work but paid less, he can claim the difference as a continuing loss.

Loss of fringe benefits   This includes fringe benefits lost both before and after the date of the hearing. Examples include: use of a company car, free or cheap accommodation, tips and mortgage allowances.

Loss of statutory industrial rights and notice period   Usually a sum is awarded to take account of the fact that the employee will have to requalify for minimum notice rights and unfair dismissal protection. The usual figure is very low – £100 was recommended in 1986.

Expenses Certain expenses can be taken into account, e.g. looking for new employment including travel, telephone calls, advertisements, removal costs, etc. In one case, £500 was awarded to cover the costs of taking a course on setting up a business.

Pensions This is the most difficult area. Loss of pension rights can be very complex – but there is a useful guide issued by the Government's Actuary Department which deals with the whole question and should always be consulted.

Despite the potential size of awards the average basic plus compensatory award in 1986–7 was only £1805.

Special award

This relates to unfair dismissal because of union or non-union activities. Beware: maximum compensation can be unlimited.

Redundancy

Redundancy payments are invested with popular myth. Large payments to coal miners have made people think all redundancy payments are large. They are not. Mandatory redundancy payments are quite low.

Is an employee within the redundancy legislation?

The redundancy laws only apply to employees, not to the self-employed (see earlier in this chapter). To qualify for redundancy an employee must satisfy the conditions stated earlier in this chapter under the heading Unfair dismissal, Qualifying conditions.

Has the employee been 'dismissed'?

The redundancy legislation only applies if an employee has been dismissed. If he resigns (unless his resignation is a constructive dismissal, see earlier in this chapter) he can claim nothing.

Voluntary redundancies

'Voluntary' redundancies can cause problems. Is a voluntary redundancy a 'dismissal'? Generally someone who volunteers to be dismissed and is then dismissed can claim redundancy.

Has the employee been dismissed by reason of redundancy?

Redundancy occurs when

- the employer closes down the business, e.g. XYZ Fabrics shuts down completely;
- the employer closes down the workplace, e.g. XYZ Fabrics shuts its Macclesfield branch;
- the employer no longer needs the employee, e.g. XYZ Fabrics stops making a certain product and no longer needs certain staff.

Normally the employee's job must have disappeared. There is no redundancy if the employer immediately engages a direct replacement (this may be unfair dismissal).

Unfair selection for redundancy

There is a form of unfair dismissal called unfair selection for redundancy. Redundancy usually makes a dismissal 'fair'. Hence a redundant employee can only claim a redundancy payment but not compensation for unfair dismissal. However, if the employee is unfairly selected for redundancy then he can claim unfair dismissal. So, what is unfair selection for redundancy?

It all depends on what criteria the employer used to select the persons being made redundant. 'Last in, first out', i.e. the last employee taken on is the first to be made redundant, is a standard criterion and is generally accepted as fair. Employers can use other standards, e.g. capability, qualifications and performance but these give the employee much more scope for arguing that the standards are unfair.

Note that a policy of making part-timers redundant first, which might seem sensible and fair, will run into problems under the Sex Discrimination legislation, as 80 per cent of part-timers are women.

The offer of another job

An employee may lose his redudancy payment if he turns down the offer of another job – it all depends on the type of job and the way in which the job is offered.

Redundancy payments

The following rules apply:

1 An employee must claim his redundancy payment in writing within six months of the end of his old job.
2 The method of calculating redundancy payments is exactly the same as for calculating the basic award for unfair dismissal, so reference should be made to exhibit 3 (page 104). The maximum redundancy payment is 30 weeks wages based on the current maximum weekly salary of £172, i.e. £5160 (this will apply to 31 March 1990).
3 Redundancy payments are tax deductible for the employer and tax free for the employee.

The duty to consult

An employer who is considering making employees redundant must give as much warning as possible to the employees concerned. If the employer fails to do this he could be found to have acted 'unreasonably' and to give rise to an 'unfair selection for redundancy' claim.

There is also a specific obligation to consult any trade unions recognized by the employer *and* the Department of Employment if the employer is planning to make a hundred or more employees redundant within a period of 90 days or to make ten employees redundant within a period of 30 days.

Time off work to look for a job

An employee with at least two years service who has been given notice of redundancy is entitled to take a reasonable amount of *paid* time off work to look for a new job or make arrangements for job training. The amount of time allowed is generally considered to be two days.

Key points

- Give suitably flexible written particulars of employment.
- Always act reasonably.
- Unfair dismissal awards and statutory redundancy payments are usually quite small.

7

Insurance

Outline

The law relating to insurance is quite complex. This chapter covers:

- insurance contracts
- compulsory insurance: employer's liability, motor vehicles
- the insurances you should have: buildings, contents, business interruption, public and product liability, professional indemnity
- the insurances you might consider: directors and officers, legal expenses, libel

Having found premises, kitted them out, purchased stock (if appropriate) and engaged staff, the new businessman needs to think about insurance. Insurance is rather like the mythical Dutch boy with his finger in the dyke. It is supposed to hold back the floodwaters of physical destruction or liabilities from swamping a business.

Law lurks behind everything in insurance; be it the legal complexities of the relationship between insurer and insured, the meaning of the risks of perils insured against or the legal liabilities which insurance is designed to cover.

You must distinguish between the many varieties of insurance available. You must take out employer's liability insurance and road traffic insurance – this is compulsory. If you purchase a property, your mortgagees will require that you insure the property against damage by fire, wind, storm and other risks. Whatever you do it is essential that you should insure your stock and assets against physical damage and your business against public liability risks.

Beyond that, your choice of insurance depends on what line of business you are in. If you are in a service industry, e.g. a solicitor or an electrician, you will need professional indemnity insurance. If you are manufacturing goods, you will need product liability insurance. In either case it is prudent to have business interruption insurance.

An introduction to the world of insurance

You can arrange most insurance policies either

- by going straight to an insurance company,
- by going via a broker.

Most of the major insurance companies cover the normal range of risks which most businesses will insure against, but you cannot be certain that the terms that company offers on each category of insurance are the best.

So you might like to employ an insurance broker. A broker has access to a wider choice of insurers or underwriters (they mean the same thing) than if you go to one insurance company. If you do use a broker you should get one thing straight. You pay him although he does not invoice for his service. He gets his fee from 'his brokerage', i.e. a form of commission paid to him by the insurer to whom he introduces the business but calculated on the value of the business. The broker is *your* agent. If he fills in the proposal form incorrectly you may be uninsured. If the error was due to his fault you could sue the broker for breach of contract (see chapter 4).

The law relating to insurance contracts

Jargon

Jargon	*Meaning*
All risks	Insurance against most forms of physical risk (except wear and tear)
Average	If you are underinsured you pay the price (see later in this chapter)

Excess | The initial part of each claim on your insurance policy which you agree to pay
Insured | The person covered by the insurance
Insurer | The person who gives the insurance
Limit of indemnity | The maximum you can recover under the policy
Premium | The price for insurance
Risk | What you insure against, e.g. fire; 'peril' means the same as risk
Sum insured | The amount at which the insured property is valued

Utmost good faith

Insurance contracts are different from normal contracts. They are contracts of 'the utmost good faith'. This means the insured has a duty to act with the 'utmost good faith' towards the insurer. In particular you must advise the insurer of all material facts relevant to your application for insurance. You must reveal anything that would influence a prudent insurer either in deciding to take on the risk or for what premium. If you fail to disclose all material facts, the insurer can escape all liability. It does not matter that you thought a fact was irrelevant; if it might have affected the mythical prudent insurer you have broken your duty. So beware. Fill in those proposal forms with care.

Average

Most insurance policies which cover property, e.g. contents, contain an average clause. This means that if you underinsure, the insurers will only be liable for a proportion of your loss.

Suppose your office contents are insured for £20,000. Their value is £30,000. Someone steals £10,000 worth of them. Applying average you recover

$$10{,}000 \times \frac{\text{£20,000(sum insured)}}{\text{£30,000(value of contents)}} = \text{£6,666}$$

Because you had only insured for two-thirds of the value of your contents you only recover two-thirds of your loss.

So, check your insurances each year. Make sure you increase the sums insured to reflect new purchases and inflation in values.

The measure of indemnity

Insurance covers you for your actual loss at the date of the accident or loss. Hence you only recover the value of the goods at that date, i.e. their second-hand value. You do not get full replacement value unless you have specifically arranged a 'new for old' or 'replacement value' policy. Of course nothing comes free. You have to pay a higher premium for the extra cover.

Excesses

Many policies are subject to an excess so as to choke off minor claims; typically the figure is £50 but can be much higher in business insurances.

Compulsory insurance

Employers' liability

The Employers' Liability (Compulsory Insurance) Act 1969 requires

> every employer carrying on a business trade or profession in Great Britain (separate legislation applies in Northern Ireland) to take out and maintain insurance with an authorized insurer against liability for bodily injury or disease sustained by his employees arising out of their employment.

- The indemnity is usually unlimited.
- A certificate of the insurance has to be displayed at the employer's premises.
- The premium is based on the estimated amount of annual wages and salaries.
- The insurance only applies to 'employees' not independent contractors (see chapter 6). Just because insurance is compulsory does not mean that the employer is automatically liable for any injury that an employee sustains as a result of his employment. The employee still has to prove that his injury was the result of

1 negligence by the employer; or
2 breach of statutory duty, e.g. breach of the Health and Safety at Work etc. Act (see chapter 6); or
3 personal negligence of fellow employees.

The amount of the premium charged varies according to what activities employees are engaged in; office workers are a much lower risk than construction site workers.

Motor insurance

Section 143(1) of the Road Traffic Act 1988 requires:

> every person who uses, or causes or permits another person to use, a motor vehicle on a road to have a policy of insurance to cover any liability which may be incurred as a result of the death of, or bodily injury to, any person or damage to property caused by, or arising out of, the use of the vehicle on a road in Great Britain.

Note: insurance is not required by law against the following risks which arise from using a motor vehicle on a road in Great Britain:

1 Liability for death or bodily injury or property damage arising out of and in the course of employment of an employee of the person insured. The reason for this exception is that employers have to insure against their liability for death or bodily injury of employees under the Employer's Liability (Compulsory Insurance) Act (see last section). Strangely enough employers are not compelled to insure against their liability for damage to their employees' property either under the 1969 or the 1988 Act, but it might be worth considering extending your insurances to cover this risk.
2 For more than £250,000 in respect of liability for damage to property (but not death or bodily injury) arising out of any one accident.
3 For damage to the owner's vehicle (in other words only 'third party' (see chapter 4) insurance is compulsory).
4 For liability for damage to goods carried for hire by the vehicle or any trailer (goods would normally be insured separately).

Certificate of motor insurance

A policy is of *no* effect under the 1988 Act unless and until the insurer *delivers* to the insured 'a certificate in the prescribed form'. The certificate is different from the policy.

Is your insurance cover wide enough?

Make sure that your insurance cover is wide enough for all your activities. The doctrine of 'utmost good faith' (see earlier in this chapter) can result in what you thought was your insurance cover being invalid. For example a policy which specifies the use as 'social domestic and pleasure purposes' does not cover a trip by the owner of a business to negotiate a contract! If a car is insured in connection with the owner's specified business, use for another business also owned by him will not be covered. So a shop owner who insures his car for his shop-owning business would not be covered if he used his car in connection with a part-time business of modelling. Do check that your proposed use is fully described in the certificate of insurance. Ensure too that employees are allowed to drive the business's vehicles (if that is what you want).

It is a criminal offence to use, cause or permit to be used a motor vehicle on a road whilst uninsured. The offence carries 6–8 penalty points. There is a special defence for employees who use an uninsured vehicle during the course of their employment without knowing it is uninsured.

The insurances you should have

Damage to buildings insurance

You will normally only have to arrange insurance for damage to your buildings if you own them. If you lease them it is normal for the landlord to insure. However, this is not always the case. For example, British Rail puts the obligation to insure any property it leases out on to the tenant.

The normal risks or perils to insure against are destruction or damage by fire, lightning, explosion, storm, tempest and flood.

If you are insuring your own buildings or just checking that your landlord's cover is sufficient under a lease you should ensure that

- the sum insured to cover the cost of rebuilding is adequate, bearing in mind the length of time it can take to get planning permission and rebuild, and the nasty habit building costs have of escalating;
- the perils insured against are wide enough to cover all possible risks – many policies, for example, do not cover subsidence which has become more widespread following dry summers;
- the policy covers not merely building costs but also professional fees, e.g. architects, surveyors, etc.

If you are letting out your building or are a tenant make sure that

- the policy covers a reasonable period (e.g. two years) loss of rent; this ties in with the rent suspension clause (see chapter 3); it means that, whilst the building is incapable of being occupied, the tenant is not obliged to pay rent; instead the landlord is paid the rent by the insurers;
- the tenant's interest is noted on the policy;
- the proceeds of the insurances are divided between the landlord and the tenant in accordance with their respective interests in the premises – this means that if the tenant has carried out extensive improvements and these are destroyed he will be reimbursed for the value of those improvements from the landlord's insurance policy; if the landlord's insurance policy does not cover this, the tenant should insure his own improvements separately.

Loss or damage to contents insurance

You will need to insure the contents of your business premises against loss or damage. This covers stocks, machinery, computers, office equipment, furnishings, motor vehicles (in addition to the compulsory insurance required under the 1988 Act) and employee's personal belongings.

You should insure against

- physical damage (e.g. fire, explosion, flood, etc.) – you will normally insure against many of the same risks as for buildings;
- theft

You may want to consider 'all risks' insurance in respect of valuable machinery or equipment. 'All risks' is a misnomer; it covers most forms of physical loss or damage other than that caused by

war
nuclear contamination
wear and tear
riot and civil commotion (e.g. in Northern Ireland)

Under an 'all risks' policy, each item insured must be specified and a separate sum insured must be allocated to it. The geographical ambit of the policy will normally be the United Kingdom but extensions can be obtained to cover movement of items abroad.

As ever, make sure you choose an adequate sum insured otherwise 'average' will strike. Ask yourself if you should insure on a replacement value basis.

Business interruption insurance

If your business premises are destroyed, be it partially or totally, your business will suffer. Not only will you have to replace your damaged premises but you will lose trading revenue. To cover this potential loss, most businesses can take out consequential loss or business interruption insurance (they mean the same). To add to the confusion, some insurers call such policies 'loss of profits'. Moreover consequential loss insurance is nothing to do with consequential loss in civil damages (see chapter 4).

Such policies generally cover not only loss of revenues but also additional expenditure which you may have reasonably to incur in consequence of the loss, damage or destruction of the premises. It will include the cost of fitting out replacement premises, increased rents, rates, lighting, heating, moving costs, etc.

The premiums for this type of insurance vary according to the risks insured against, the level of indemnity and the length of cover. It would be normal to insure against the same risks as are covered by the building insurance policy. The length of cover after the loss is known as the indemnity period and is a matter of individual choice, but should not be less than 12 months.

Public liability insurance

The purpose of taking out public liability insurance is to cover the business against its liability to third parties for causing death, personal injury or damage to their property. The public liability policy excludes risks covered by other types of policy, e.g. employer's liability and road traffic insurance. The two broad fields covered by a public liability policy are

1 risks arising from the ownership, occupation or management of premises;
2 risks arising from the activities of employees to third parties.

Briefly these are as follows.

Premises risks

1 Escape of dangerous things from your land/buildings, e.g. pollution.
2 Dangerous premises: under the Occupier's Liability Act 1957 the occupier of any premises owes a duty of care to his visitor to see that the visitor is reasonably safe in using the premises for the purpose for which he is invited. Hence by taking on a lease or buying a freehold, a business person is under a duty to ensure that the premises are reasonably safe. If they are not and someone is injured or their property damaged, he can be sued.
Under the Health and Safety at Work etc. Act, duties are owed to visitors (as opposed to employees) who visit premises – the risk of breaking these obligations is also covered by public liability insurance.

Employees' activities risks

Risks arising from the activities of employees and agents are known by lawyers as 'vicarious liability'.

An employer is liable for the negligent act or omissions of his employees which cause death, bodily injury or damage to property during the course of their employment. Beware: for these purposes an employee has a much wider meaning than in employment law (see chapter 6) or tax law (see chapter 8). For the purposes of *vicarious* liability a person is treated as an employee if the insured had the right to control the way in which the negligent deed was done.

The public liability policy is not all-embracing. It excludes many forms of liability which are covered by other insurance policies, e.g.

- employer's liability;
- motor vehicles;
- liability arising under contract;
- professional negligence;
- product liability.

The first two and last two of these are discussed in more detail elsewhere in this chapter.

It is best to select a decent level of indemnity for your public liability policy. This type of insurance is quite cheap; so £1m worth of cover should not cost too much and is well worth taking out.

Product liability insurance

In chapter 4 the obligations imposed on producers or importers of certain types of goods under the Consumer Protection Act 1987, the Sale of Goods Act 1979 or under the common law rules of negligence were considered. Claims under these Acts or in negligence could bankrupt a business. Take an example. Say a partnership produces a defective product. A consumer sustains serious long-term injury from using the product and sues the partners. The costs of defending the action and of meeting any court award or out-of-court settlement could run into hundreds of thousands of pounds. Such costs could bankrupt the partners and all their personal wealth or assets would be lost. If the business was conducted through a limited company, although the directors would not be at risk of losing their personal possessions, an uninsured claim could force the limited company into liquidation. And if a claim is made in the United States where juries have a tendency to award enormous damages for the most trifling injury, the potential liabilities can be huge.

To cover against these risks a business can take out a product liability insurance policy. Such cover is not cheap. Premiums depend on such obvious factors as the amount of turnover, the nature of the business, where goods are exported to, the manufacturing process, etc. If you are manufacturing goods, the insurers will almost certainly wish to inspect the premises.

The policy will contain certain exclusions, e.g. the cost of actually replacing a defective product – this insurance is product *liability*, i.e. liability for loss, damage or bodily injury arising from defective products. It does not cover any costs of replacing a defective product. Such insurance *can* be obtained (at a price) – it is called product guarantee insurance.

Professional indemnity insurance

By the Supply of Goods and Services Act 1982 and common law, suppliers of service are under obligation to use reasonable skill and care in carrying out their duties (see chapter 4 for more details). Professionals are under a higher duty.

The title 'professional indemnity' insurance is a misnomer. Insurance cover against the risks that a supplier of services may not comply with his or her legal duties is *not* only available for what are usually termed 'professionals'. Insurance can be obtained for plumbers, electricians, estate agents and brokers as well as the 'true' professionals, e.g. solicitors, accountants, doctors, architects, etc. In each case (unless there is a scheme, as for solicitors and doctors) premiums are calculated according to the nature of the business, the turnover, where the business is conducted, the number of unqualified staff, etc.

As with product liability insurance, premiums are high, especially if you carry on business in the United States.

The insurances you should consider taking out

Director's and officer's liability insurance

This will become an increasingly popular form of insurance. There has been some doubt as to whether a limited company could pay the premiums as the company is not the beneficiary of the policy. That uncertainty has been resolved by the Companies Act 1989 which permits limited companies to take out such policies and pay the premiums.

The risks insured under the policy are all claims arising from the insured person's acts or omissions in carrying out his or her duties as a director or officer of a company. Typical examples of risks include

1 negligent performance of duties;
2 liability for torts of the company;
3 breach of the Companies Acts: the Insolvency Act 1986 introduced wrongful trading (see chapter 11); this provides that directors of a limited company that goes into insolvent liquidation can be made to make a payment from their personal assets to the creditors of the company; as a result this form of insurance is becoming more popular.

There are a number of exclusions from the typical policy including liabilities arising from fraud or under guarantees or warranties given by the director.

Legal expenses insurance

Taking legal proceedings is expensive. Even if, at the end of the day, you win and get most of your costs back, you still have a major financial commitment whilst fighting the case, and until the judge or arbitrator gives his decision you do not know for certain if you will win. The fear of legal costs puts many people off fighting claims. At times this can be sensible – if it deters the petty claim, well and good. But the fear of costs can deter someone with a genuine claim or grievance contesting a matter. To plug this particular hole you can take out legal expenses insurance.

There are various types of legal expenses insurance. Some are very specialized and give cover solely in respect of employment issues (see chapter 6). Insurers arrange telephone advice on handling complaints, disciplinary procedure, etc., as well as actually providing lawyers to contest tribunal or court proceedings. Some are more general and give an indemnity for a wide range of legal costs. There is a limit to the amount of expenses that can be claimed in any year. The cover may be subject to certain exclusions, e.g. conveyancing, defamation, disputes with the Inland Revenue. This form of insurance is not very expensive and is well worth considering.

Libel insurance

If you print or publish books, magazines, journals, etc., you may need libel insurance.

Fidelity insurance

This insures against employees stealing the firm's money – beware that if you have this form of cover you almost invariably have to take up a *written* reference on each new member of staff who handles money.

Your insurance policies and others

A number of different people may be interested in your insurance policies:

1 Your landlord: you may have to insure the premises leased to you.
2 Your mortgagees: if you mortgage property the mortgagee will wish to make sure it is adequately insured. Depending on what property is mortgaged this can cover buildings (even if the landlord arranges the cover), stock, plant and machinery, goods in transit and consequential loss. The mortgagee may want 'key man' cover. This, as its (albeit sexist) name implies, is an insurance policy on the life and health of a 'key' or important employee (if he or she should die or be unable to work permanently, the business will suffer). The insurance protects the business from the loss of revenue caused by the absence of the key individual. They may also want their interest as mortgagees noted on the insurance policies.
3 Your finance company: if you hire purchase, hire or lease equipment, in the tiny small print of the contract (if you have the patience to read it), you will invariably find an obligation on the hiree or lessee (*not* the owner) to insure the equipment against 'all risks' and to note the interest of the owner on the policy. So each time you acquire any equipment on hire purchase or lease you should notify your insurers with full details of the equipment concerned.

4 Your investors: if you take in shareholders they may wish to see that their investment is protected by product liability or professional indemnity insurance as well as 'key man' cover. A director may want director's and officer's liability insurance cover.
5 Your employees may demand pensions or medical expenses insurance or permanent health insurance.

Conclusion

It is easy to imagine that all types of disaster might strike and that you should take out extensive insurance against the widest range of risks for the maximum sum insured. If you do, you'll probably spend most of your working capital! So before deciding on whether to take out insurance cover and the amount of cover, answer the following questions first:

- Is this insurance obligatory?
- Is this insurance necessary? Is it prudent to take it out? Does the person recommending it understand the business?
- What is the premium? Is there an alternative quotation? (Remember there are lots of insurance companies all, in theory, competing for your business.)
- Has the proposal form been completed in full? (Remember: utmost good faith.)
- What risks are covered by the policy?
- What risks are excluded?
- What are the conditions of the policy? (e.g. about storage of stock, safekeeping of money and valuables, no storage of high explosives, etc.)

Each year, about two months before the insurance policies are due for renewal, you should review them with your insurer or broker to make sure that the business is adequately insured both as regards

- level of cover;
- risks covered.

During the year remember to

1 promptly notify insurers of all claims under any insurance policy;
2 promptly advise them of any significant change in the risk, e.g. have you started storing liquid nitrogen?

Key points

- Employer's liability and Road Traffic Act insurances are compulsory.
- Many contracts may oblige you to insure property, e.g. leases, mortgages, hire purchase.
- You should consider reducing some of your risks by having some other types of insurance, e.g. product liability.

8

Taxation

Outline

Your responsibilities as far as tax is concerned are very important and this chapter examines the issues you need to consider at the very outset of trading. These include:

- sole traders and partnerships
- limited companies and tax
- capital gains tax
- employees and PAYE
- National Insurance
- VAT

The tax man cometh well before you have profits. PAYE, National Insurance and VAT all have to be paid regardless of profits. So you need to know about certain tax matters from your very first day of trading.

To some extent the taxes you pay depend on how your business is organized. Limited companies pay corporation tax on their profits whilst sole traders and partnerships pay income tax on theirs. A partner's or sole trader's income tax bill is calculated under schedule D, which is different from schedule E which applies to employees. VAT applies to all businesses with a taxable turnover of over £25,400 (this is the 1990 figure, the limit changes each year at the Budget).

National Insurance contributions vary depending on whether you are employed or self-employed.

Tax rates

Before starting you must be aware of the following.

- Tax rates are reviewed annually in the Budget. The 1990–1 rates are

Income tax

	Rate (%)	Total tax
Taxable income		
£20,700	25	5175
over £20,700	40	
Income tax allowances		
personal allowance		
married couple's		1720
single		3005

Companies

	Rate (%)
Full corporation tax	35
Small companies	25
Capital gains tax (individuals)	
first £20,700	25
over £20,700	40

The first £5000 of capital gains are tax free for an individual.

- You or your accountant should notify the local tax office, on Form 41G, that you have started business.
- If you have given up your previous employment you should send your P45 to the local inspector.
- You will have to start keeping adequate financial records.
- This is a very brief introduction to a number of very complex topics. Do not think you are an expert even if you can understand this chapter! You should take professional advice on tax matters from an accountant or a solicitor.
- There are some useful pieces of information freely available. In particular; ask your local DSS/Inland Revenue office for a copy of P4 'New Employer's Starter Pack'. This will be referred to at various points in this chapter.

Sole traders and partnerships

Tax on profits

Income tax is payable on the profits of a 'trade, profession or vocation'. A 'trade' includes manufacturing, retailing, wholesaling and all kinds of trading ventures. A 'profession' is defined as an occupation requiring special skills (e.g. solicitor, architect). A 'vocation' has been defined as the way that a person passes his life (e.g. actor, author, composer, singer).

What 'profits' are taxable?

The profits on which tax is paid under schedule D are found after deducting certain allowable business expenses and making other adjustments to your trading profits. Note that:

- only those expenses *'wholly and exclusively* incurred for the purposes of the trade, profession or vocation' are deductible;
- you *cannot* deduct capital expenditure, e.g. purchase of a car, but there are certain allowances (see later in this chapter).

What are 'allowable business expenses'?

Some examples are as follows (this is *not* an exhaustive list).

- Cost of goods bought for resale.
- Cost of raw materials used for manufacturing.
- Wages and salaries paid to employees (including employer's National Insurance contributions).
- Pensions paid to former employees and contributions to pensions for current employees.
- Running costs of premises: light, heating, rent, rates, insurance, cleaning, repairs, etc.
- Printing, postage and stationery costs.
- Repairs to plant and machinery.
- Insurances.
- Advertising/public relations.
- Legal and accountancy fees of a revenue nature, e.g. audit fees or

advice on a contract but not on acquisition of a capital item, e.g. a property purchase.

- Travelling expenses (but not the costs of travelling from home to business, unless you work from home).
- Running expenses of motor vehicles excluding whatever proportion is attributable to private use.
- Interest charges (but not repayments of loans).
- The interest element of hire purchase charges.
- Leasing payments (this is limited to the retail cost equivalent of a car of £8000).
- Bad debts which prove irrecoverable.

Note: it is necessary to agree with the Inland Revenue the proportion of your motor car expenses and any other items which are used for both business and private use. You or your accountant could do this; it is sensible to establish these apportionments early on if you can.

Stock

Stocks of raw materials, unsold goods and work in progress have to be valued at the end of each accounting period, to avoid strange results in the business's accounts. If the purchase costs of all stocks are taken in one year, even if those stocks have not been used, this deflates the profits in that year. However, in the next year there would be no deduction from the profits in that year for the stock paid for in the previous year. Hence profits would be very high. To avoid such dramatic swings, stocks are valued at the end of each accounting period.

The stock is valued at the lower of its cost or net realizable value. The value of trading stock unsold at the end of one accounting period is entered into the account of that year as a receipt. It is also entered into the account of the second period as an expense. It is thus 'sold' from one year's account to the next.

Capital allowances

You are not normally allowed to deduct from your taxable profits the cost or depreciation of capital assets. This can be very confusing as your accountant will depreciate assets in your accounts. This depreciation is *not* deductible for tax purposes. But you can deduct capital allowances on the cost of certain assets used in your business or profession. If you use the asset partly for private and partly for business purposes the allowance is apportioned in a ratio agreed with your inspector of taxes.

Capital allowances on plant and machinery

This is a sweeper phrase which is much wider than you may think. Usually it is the most important capital allowance. It includes furniture, office fittings, computers, industrial plant and machinery. The capital allowance on plant and machinery is

- 25 per cent writing down allowance each year on a reducing balance.

Using, for example, the purchase of a computer for £10,000

Year 1 writing down allowance $10,000 \times 25\% = 2500$
Year 2 writing down allowance $(10,000 - 2500)$ $7500 \times 25\% = 1875$
Year 3 writing down allowance $(7500 - 1875)$ $5525 \times 25\% = 1406$
Year 4 writing down allowance $(5525 - 1406)$ $4218 \times 25\% = 1054$
and so on

If you dispose of an item, the allowance stops. The allowance may be claimed on new or second-hand items.

If you buy more than one asset the assets are put into a 'pool' at their cost price and the 25 per cent writing down allowance is applied to the assets in the pool.

Cars

There are separate rules for cars. A car used in your business will get a 25% writing down allowance if it costs less than £8000. If it costs more than £8000, capital allowances are restricted to £8000.

Hire purchase

If you buy plant and machinery on hire purchase you get a capital allowance on the proportion of the instalment which relates to *capital*. For example, you buy a machine on HP; capital cost £2000, interest £900 over three years, period three years. You get the writing down allowances:

Year 1 25% × 2000 $\qquad$ = £500
Year 2 25% × 1500 $\quad$ (2000 − 500) = £375
Year 3 25% × 1125 $\quad$ (1500 − 375) = £281.25

As mentioned earlier the interest (£300 per year) can be offset against profits as a business expense.

Other capital allowances

There are other forms of capital allowances, notably:

- 100 per cent initial allowance for new commercial buildings in enterprise zones;
- 20 per cent initial allowance for new hotel buildings plus 4% writing down allowance;
- 100 per cent allowance for capital expenditure on scientific research for the purpose of your trade.

There are a number of others. Your accountant should be able to advise you.

Calculating your taxable profits

1 Take your profit figure from your accounts (audited or otherwise), say $\qquad$ £10,000
2 Add back any non tax deductible expenses that have been included in your accounts and thereby reduced profits, e.g. depreciation, say $\qquad$ £1,000

£11,000

3 Deduct your capital allowances, say £2000.
4 Taxable profit = £9000.
5 Tax bill = £9000 × 25% = £2250.

But, can I claim any other tax relief before I pay the tax bill? Answer? 'yes, if you have losses or unused personal allowances'.

Offsetting losses against profits

If you make a loss in one accounting period you can carry it forward and set it off against profits in subsequent years. The profits and loss must be made in the same trade, profession or vocation. For example:

Year 1 = loss   £10,000
Year 2 = profit £8,000
Year 3 = profit £12,000

The loss from year 1 wipes out any tax liability in year 2 and reduces the taxable profits in year 3 to £10,000. You must elect to carry losses forward within two years of the end of the tax year to which it relates.

Loss in a new business

Mention was made in chapter 1 of the Taxes Act 1988, s. 381, which gives a special relief if you carry on business as a sole trader or in partnership. If you make a loss in your first year of tax assessment or in any of the next three years you can offset the losses against your income for the three years of assessment prior to the year in which the losses are made, taking the earliest first. Phew! What does this mean? It means that you can make a tax repayment claim. The Inland Revenue repays to you tax you have previously paid if you offset losses against that tax. Hence, if you open a new business on 1 January 1989,

Year 1   1989/90 you lose £20,000
Year 2   1990/91 you lose £10,000

1986/87 you earned £70,000
       Your top rate of tax was 60%
1987/8 you earned £75,000
       your top rate of tax was 60%

For year 1 you can offset your loss of £20,000 against your 1986/87 income. You will get a tax repayment of £20,000 × 60% = £12,000.

For year 2 you can claim tax back of £10,000 × 60% = £6,000. Hence you get £18,000 back from the Revenue – 60 per cent of your losses.

Note that this benefit will be limited to 40 per cent once the 40 per cent maximum tax level has been in force for three years, i.e. after 6 April 1991.

How is tax calculated?

Sole traders and partnerships pay tax on what is called the 'preceding year basis'. Understanding this is made more difficult by the fact that the government's tax year begins on 6 April each year. The reason for this is that government finances used to run from 25 March (Lady Day) which was one of the quarter days for paying rent. In 1752 the government adopted the Gregorian calendar which was more accurate than the Julian calendar which had by then 'lost' eleven days. So rather than lose eleven days revenue the government extended its financial year by 11 days to 6 April!

Under the preceding year basis, tax is charged on the profits of the accounting year preceding the tax year of assessment. What a mouthful.

Thus if a business's accounts run from January 1988 to 31 December 1988 the profits from those accounts are charged to tax in the tax year 6 April 1989 to 5 April 1990.

In the accountant's jargon, the business's 1988 financial year precedes the 1989/90 tax year and so it is the profits from the 1988 financial year which are taxed in the next tax year (1989/90).

You can therefore see that if a business's accounts ran from 10 April 1987 to 9 April 1988 that period precedes the tax year 6 April 1989 to 5 April 1990. Hence the business would pay tax in the tax year 1989/90 based on profits earned almost two years previously in 1987 to 1988. If profits are rising, this gives the business a considerable advantage as its tax bill will be lower than its current profits might indicate. However, if profits are falling, this can be disastrous. The business will have less cash but will be paying tax based on the higher profits from previous years. This risk can be dealt with by keeping a proper tax reserve fund available to pay tax as and when needed.

The illustration above of running the financial year of the business from 10 April to 9 April is somewhat extreme. However, 30 April is a very common financial year end. But beware. The preceding year basis has been criticized and may be changed.

Opening years

- The preceding year basis will not work in the first few years. Hence in the first tax year the assessment is based on profits (or losses) from the starting date to the following 5 April. So, a business starts on 5 May 1988 and prepares accounts as at 5 May 1989.

  Profits are £10,000.

  The apportioned profits for the tax year 5 April 1988 to 5 April 1989 will be

$$\frac{11}{12} \times 10,000 = £9166$$

- The assessment for the second year is based on the profits (or losses) for the first 12 months. Hence, in the example, the assessment for the tax year 1989/90 will be based on the profits for the first complete year, i.e. to 5 May 1989.

- The assessment for the third year is based on the preceding year, i.e. again the profits for the period to 5 May 1989 will be used to calculate the tax bill for the tax year 1990/91.

Thus you can see that if you make a loss in the first year's accounts this will serve as the basis of tax assessment for three tax years. This can then tie in with a tax recovery claim as mentioned earlier. Note: the tax payer can elect to pay tax on the actual profits in the second and third tax years (though not one of them alone) if he so wishes.

Closing down

To some extent the Revenue can get their revenge. If the trade profession or vocation is stopped permanently the Revenue apply the following rules:

- for the tax year in which the business stopped, tax is charged on the actual profits.
- They have the right to re-open the tax assessments for the previous two years and charge more tax on any excess of the actual profits in those years (taken as a pair) when compared with

the profits used for calculating tax for those years (which will have been done on the preceding year basis).

When is tax paid?

Tax under schedule D, case I and II, is paid in two instalments. On 1 January in the year of assessment and the following 1 July. Hence, returning to the last example, in tax year 1990/91

Taxable profits = £10,000
Tax at 25% = £2500
this will be paid: £1250 on 1 January 1992
£1250 on 1 July 1992

Note: Your tax return should be sent in by 31 October in each year. If not, the Revenue may charge interest on the tax due (even if this has not been assessed). In the example your return for 1990/91 must be in by 31 October 1991.

Partnerships

Special rules apply to partnerships. The tax assessment is made on the partners in their profit sharing ratios. So if a partner takes 50 per cent of the profits he is assessed for 50 per cent of the tax. But the partners are jointly liable for the partnership's tax bill. This means that all the partners can be sued for all the partnership tax bill and judgment enforced against any of them, without reference to the profit sharing ratios. This is why it is important in any partnership to have proper rules about reserving money for tax in an account from which money can only be withdrawn with the authority of all partners.

Partnership changes

If there is a change in partners the partnership is treated as having come to an end. This could be disastrous. It allows the Inland Revenue to re-open the tax assessments for the previous two years (see the section entitled 'Closing down'). You can get round this by making what is called a continuation election. All the partners (new and old) have to sign the election within two years of the change in the partnership. This allows the partnership to be treated as continuing. Hence the 'closing down' rules do not apply. But you cannot force a partner to sign a continuation election. You should cover this in your partnership agreement.

Limited companies

Tax on a limited company's profits

The tax regime for limited companies is in a number of ways different from that for sole traders or partnerships.

- Companies pay corporation tax.
- Corporation tax rates for the corporation tax year 1990/91 are

  35% on taxable profits over £1,000,000
  25% on taxable profits under £200,000

  On profits between £200,000 and £1,000,000 tax is charged at the 35 per cent rate less a fixed fraction by which they fall short of £1,000,000, which gives a marginal rate of 37½ per cent.
- To complicate matters further, the corporation tax year starts on 1 April (not 6 April as for other taxes).

What 'taxable profits' are caught by corporation tax? Answer: the calculation of taxable profits for corporation tax purposes is almost the same as for sole traders and partnerships, namely

- allowable expenses have to be wholly and exclusively for the purposes of the trade;
- capital allowances apply.

Dividends

Limited companies can pay dividends out of distributable profits (see chapter 2 for further details). Distributable profits are found after paying the tax due on those profits.

If a limited company paid a dividend to a shareholder, he would then pay income tax on the total dividend received. For example,

Company's pre-tax profits are £100,000	
Tax at 25%	£25,000
Net of tax	£75,000

The company pays all this out by dividend to Bloggs, its 100 per cent shareholder. Bloggs would then pay income tax at 40 per cent on £75,000, i.e. £30,000. On the profits of £100,000 the tax paid would be

Company (25% of £100,000)	£25,000
Bloggs (40% of £75,000)	£30,000
Total (effectively 55% of £100,000)	£55,000

To stop this double tax charge, companies pay 'advance corporation tax'. In the example, the company would not pay £75,000 to Bloggs as a dividend. Instead it becomes liable to pay advance corporation tax (ACT) of $^{25}/_{75}$ on the £75,000 which equals £25,000. Thus the total distribution by the company is £100,000 with £25,000 going to ACT (equivalent to basic rate income tax).

ACT must be paid over to the Revenue by the company on an ACT accounting date, i.e. 31 March, 30 June, 30 September, 31 December, or the company's financial year end, if not one of those dates. But the company can deduct the ACT from its corporation tax bill.

Hence the company's corporation tax bill is

Due to Inland Revenue (25% of £100,000)	£25,000
Less ACT paid	£25,000
Balance of corporation tax due	nil

Bloggs receives £100,000 (i.e. cash of £75,000 plus £25,000 ACT). As he has already paid ACT on the dividend, he can set this against his tax liability so he is only due to pay higher rate tax on it, i.e.

40% × £100,000	£40,000
Less ACT paid	£25,000
Balance due	£15,000

Hence under the ACT system the total tax paid is

Company (ACT)	£25,000
Bloggs	£15,000
Total	£40,000

This is £15,000 less than would be paid if first the company paid corporation tax on profits and Bloggs paid income tax on the dividends.

What financial periods of profits are taxed?

Corporation tax (CT) is not assessed on the preceding year basis. This is a major difference between limited companies and sole traders and partnerships. Instead CT is charged on the actual profits of each accounting period. This will usually coincide with the periods for which the company prepares its annual accounts but it cannot exceed 12 months.

For example, a company prepares its accounts for the year 1 July 1988 to 30 June 1989. Its profits were £100,000. It pays CT as follows:

CT year 1 April 1988 to 31 March 1989   CT rate = 25%
CT year 1 April 1989 to 31 March 1990   CT rate = 25%
CT for year 1 April 1988 to 31 March 1989
$$= £100,000 \times \frac{9}{12} \times 25\% = £18,750$$
CT for year 1 April 1989 to 31 March 1990
$$= £100,000 \times \frac{3}{12} \times 25\% = £6,250$$

Hence with CT, the CT rate for each tax year is charged on the profits of the company for that year.

When is CT paid?

CT has to be paid nine months after the date of the accounting period. Hence in the example, the accounting period ended on 30 June 1989. CT must be paid on 31 March 1990. However, if an assessment has not been issued, no CT need be paid until the assessment is issued. The company then has 30 days from the date of issue within which to pay. The Keith Report has recommended tightening this up so all CT has to be paid within nine months of the end of the accounting period, even if no assessment has been issued. This proposal is unlikely to come into effect before 1993.

Capital gains tax (CGT)

However your business is constituted it will be liable to pay tax in respect of chargeable gains made on the disposal of certain assets. Limited companies pay corporation tax, everyone else pays CGT.

Only capital gains made on the disposal of certain assets are charged to tax:

- land, buildings, stocks, shares, antiques, goodwill, plant and machinery, ships, aircraft, vehicles (but not private motor cars);
- options;
- any currency other than sterling.

Exempt assets

Certain assets are exempt but do not be too hopeful! The following list is not exhaustive. Exemptions cover an esoteric group of assets including private motor vehicles, your main private residence, compensation or damages and payments for personal injuries.

What is a disposal?

A disposal occurs much more often than you might think, notably

- the outright sale of an asset or part of it;
- the gift of an asset or part of it;
- if an asset is destroyed, e.g. by fire;
- if a capital sum is received for giving up a right, e.g. surrendering a lease.

The date at which the gain is made can be crucial. It is the date of the sale contract not when the contract is completed if this is different.

CGT is payable on gains. The name of the tax is absolutely correct. In calculating the capital gain you can deduct the following from the proceeds of sale or the market value (whichever happens to be appropriate).

1 The original cost or value at acquisition ('the base value').
2 Capital expenditure for improvements or enhancements during period of ownership.
3 Your incidental costs of acquisition and disposal, e.g. solicitor's fees, stamp duty.
4 The indexation allowance, which is designed to increase the base value in line with inflation so that CGT is charged only on genuine gains and not on inflation. Your accountant will be able to work out the precise formula.
5 If you owned an asset before 31 March 1982, its base value is automatically taken to be its value at that date.
6 Any capital losses, e.g. on selling shares when the stock market crashes.

Calculation of CGT – sole traders and partners

Having worked out the net taxable capital gain as above, you then deduct £5000 (this is the annual exemption for the 1990/91 tax year).

Hence, if you have a net taxable gain, after making all adjustments, of £50,000

Net taxable gain	£50,000
Deduct annual exemption	£5,000
Net figure chargeable to CGT	£45,000

CGT is chargeable either at 25 per cent or 40 per cent.

If your income liable to income tax exceeds the basic income tax band of £20,700, the entire gain will be taxed at 40 per cent. If you have not used up all your basic rate income tax band, the position is as follows. Say your taxable income is £15,700. You have £20,700 − £15,700 = £5,000 left of the 25 per cent basic rate income tax band unused. To return to the example above. You will therefore pay *CGT* as follows:

£5,000 × 25%	£1,250
£40,000 × 40%	£16,000
Total CGT	£17,250

When do sole traders and partners pay CGT?

CGT is due to be paid on the later of either

- 30 days after the date the Revenue issue an assessment; or
- 1 December in the year after the end of the tax year in which the gain was made, i.e.

Tax year: 6 April 1988 to 5 April 1989
Gain made: 1 January 1989, i.e. in tax year 1988/89
CGT due 1 December 1989

Special reliefs

You should know about two particular reliefs.

Losses on unquoted shares in trading companies

This relief applies to a UK limited trading company which

1 is not quoted on the USM or Stock Exchange; and
2 has traded for at least six years or, if less, from within a year of its incorporation; and
3 is a qualifying company, namely it has not traded in land, shares, commodity futures.

If you or your spouse make a loss on your investment in shares in such a trading company you can choose to get relief from *income* tax on the loss. In other words you can offset your capital loss on the shares against any income tax you may have to pay. This is most unusual. Normally capital losses have to be set against capital gains.

Roll over relief

If you dispose of an asset which has been used in the course of your business and further business assets are purchased within one year before and three years after the sale, you can apply for 'roll over' relief. By this the gain on the disposal is deducted from the cost of the new business assets effectively reducing your acquisition cost. Thus, the gain is 'rolled over' and no CGT is paid until the new assets are disposed of. Note that this does not apply to motor cars or vans. The new plant has to be 'fixed'.

If the new asset is a wasting asset (i.e. it does not have a predictable life of more than 50 years) it must be replaced by a non-wasting asset within ten years. If not the 'rolled over' gain becomes chargeable to CGT and you get a tax bill based on the original gain.

Limited companies and CGT

Limited companies pay corporation tax on their capital gains. Their liability for capital gains tax is calculated as set out above. But the rate of tax they pay is their corporation tax rate, i.e. 25 per cent or 35 per cent depending on whether they are 'small' or not (see earlier in this chapter). Limited companies pay their capital gains tax bill at the same time as their corporation tax bill (see earlier in this chapter).

Employees and PAYE

However you set up your business, if you employ any staff you will have to deal with PAYE and schedule E tax. This applies to employees' income. If you are a partner or sole trader, you are treated as self-employed and pay tax under schedule D (see earlier in this chapter). If you set up a limited company and become a full-time director, you will be treated as an employee and pay PAYE. If you establish yourself as a sole trader, in partnership or as a limited company and employ staff they will be subject to PAYE.

Self-employed?

For the difference between an employee and a self-employed person see chapter 6. Err on the side of caution in treating people as self-employed. The part-time secretary or receptionist may claim to be self-employed, but if the Inland Revenue or DSS disagrees, you could end up paying income tax, employee's NI and employer's NI on the gross salary you have paid.

For example, you treat someone as self-employed and pay them £10,000 gross. The Inland Revenue claims that person is not self-employed and that you should have operated PAYE. You could end up paying the following.

1 Gross up £10,000 to the figure on which you should have charged basic rate income tax at 25 per cent plus employee's NI at 9 per cent = 34 per cent.

$$\frac{£10,000 \times 100}{66} = £15,151$$

2 Charge income tax and employer's NI at 34 per cent on £15,151 = £5,151
3 Charge employer's NI contributions at 10.45 per cent on £15,151 = £1,583.

The total demand could be

	£5,151	PAYE plus employee's NI
	£1,583	employer's NI
Total	£6,734	

Be warned: PAYE/NI audits are becoming quite common. The Revenue has found that they are a very effective way of raising revenue.

The Inland Revenue and DSS both claim to have one particular officer in each area who can answer questions about self-employed status. So check first, if someone claims to be 'self-employed'. Alternatively you could ask your solicitor or accountant.

What employees' income is taxable?

This list is not exhaustive, but includes

normal salary or wages
overtime
holiday pay
sick pay, including SSP
cost of living allowances
luncheon vouchers (if over 15p per day)
Christmas or other cash gifts
bonuses
commission
value of goods or shares given free to employee
fringe benefits (see below)
maternity pay

Fringe benefits

Fringe benefits mean any benefit from employment not paid as a salary. If an employee earns more than £8500 per annum including fringe benefits or is a director, then the fringe benefits are taxed on the actual cost of providing the benefits. If you have employees in this class, you must file a Form P11D with the Revenue each year by 1 June of the relevant tax year.

The topic is complex. The Revenue booklet 'Notes on Expenses Payments and Benefits for Directors and Certain Employees' (ref. 480) runs to 60 pages of tight print. You are spared that here. But if you need more detail that is as good a place as any to get free information – if your eyesight can take the print.

The types of benefits which have to be listed are

- cars owned or hired by the employer where the employee is allowed to use these for private journeys;
- entertainment expenses;
- travelling and subsistences – fares, hotels, meals etc.;
- private insurance cover, e.g. BUPA;
- educational assistance;
- interest free or subsidized loans to employees.

The value of these fringe benefits are assessed and the employee is sent a tax bill.

Motor car

Special tax rules apply to motor cars supplied by the employer to a director or a 'higher paid' employee (i.e. over £8500 per annum). Your accountant should be able to advise you on this.

PAYE

Most schedule E tax is collected under PAYE which covers both basic and higher rate tax. The Revenue uses employers as its tax collectors. As an employer you have to understand and administer the PAYE system. You should consult the Inland Revenue/DSS Starter Pack (see earlier in this chapter).

Payment

Many new businesses hope they can use the Inland Revenue as a banker by delaying paying PAYE. The Inland Revenue get very concerned about this. PAYE is due in by the 19th of the following month. So PAYE deducted for April salaries has to be paid by 19 May.

Payment is made not to your local tax office but to the collector of taxes. Your local tax office (or accountant) will advise you where this is.

Records

You must keep PAYE records either on your own records, including a computer, or on the official Deductions Working Sheet. The Revenue has the power to investigate. PAYE audits have become increasingly common and these have revealed widespread maladministration in PAYE with consequent claims for arrears and fines.

PAYE returns

You must complete a P35 plus a P14 for each employee at the end of each tax year and send it to the local tax office with the Deductions Working Sheet (P11(87)).

National Insurance contributions (NICs)

Administering PAYE may be bad but NICs are worse. You must distinguish

- NICs for the self-employed; and
- NICs for the employed.

NICs and the self-employed

The self-employed (sole traders, partners, independent contractors, etc.) pay two types of NICs (April 1990 rates):

1 Class 2: current rate £4.55 per week, i.e. £236.60 per annum.
2 Class 4: 6.3 per cent earned income (see earlier in this chapter) between £5,450 and £18,200. The annual maximum is thus £803.25 (6.3 per cent of 12,750).

Class 2 NICs are paid direct to the DSS. Class 4 NICs are collected by the Revenue when you pay your income tax bill on 1 January and 1 July in each year (see earlier in this chapter). Half the Class 4 NIC is allowable as a business expense when computing trading profits for tax purposes. Rates are set each year in the Budget.

Self-employed NICs are quite low. The other side of the coin is that the self-employed get fewer state benefits being ineligible for

- unemployment benefit;
- statutory sick pay;
- state earnings related pensions.

NICs and employees

NICs for employees are made up of

1 The employer's share;
2 the employee's share.

These are called Class 1 contributions. Class 1 contributions are charged on 'gross' pay.

Earnings limits

The employee's contributions are subject to an upper and lower earnings limit. The rates vary depending on whether or not the employee belongs to the state related pension scheme (SERPS) or has their own personal pension plan, or belongs to an approved fund operated by his employer. If he has his own personal pension plan, he is *not* 'contracted out'. Employees who are part of an approved pension plan *are* 'contracted out' and pay lower NICs. Exhibit 4 gives contribution rates for those not contracted out.

There is no upper earnings limit for employer's contributions contracted out.

Exhibit 4 Class 1 NICs: Not contracted out (1990–1 rates)

Weekly earnings band	Employees	Employers
Under £46	Nil	Nil
£46–79.99 (2% of first £46)	9%	5%
£80–124.99 (2% of first £46)	9%	7%
£125–174.99 (2% of first £46)	9%	9%
£175–350 (2% of first £46)	9%	10.45%

Employer's NICs

The rates of employer's NICs are set out in exhibit 4. The crucial point is that the 10.45 per cent employer's contribution is not subject to an upper limit. This means that salaries and bonuses always attract the employer's NIC contribution. Hence in private limited companies where the full-time directors are also share-holders, it is sensible to pay out any surplus by a dividend rather than salaries and/or bonuses, as dividends will not attract the 10.45 per cent employer's NICs whereas salaries and/or bonuses will.

Returns

At the end of each tax year you have to make an end of year return to the *inspector of taxes*.

NICs – conclusion

As can be seen, employer's and employee's NICs total much more than self-employed NICs. This is another factor when considering whether or not to start a business as a sole trader or partnership or limited company.

Value added tax (VAT)

VAT is a sales tax. The ultimate consumer, i.e. the person who purchases the finished product in a shop or buys a meal in a restaurant, bears all the tax. Along the business chain, businesses pay and charge VAT on the 'value added' at each stage of the chain.

But businesses are not out of pocket over VAT; they get a credit for the VAT paid and they *charge* customers for VAT. They collect VAT for the Customs and Excise. The only occasions when VAT costs a business money is if the business is wholly or partly exempt from VAT or if it is due to collect some VAT from a customer who goes bust. Then the business has to get the Customs and Excise to waive that VAT which the business charged but did not collect.

An example might help (VAT at 15 per cent):

	Price (ex. VAT) £	*VAT* £	*Paid to Customs* £
A imports raw materials	100	15	15
A sells finished goods to B	300	45	
A accounts for VAT to Customs (£45 − £15)			30
B sells to C	400	60	
B accounts for VAT to Customs (£60 − £45)			15
C sells goods to D	800	120	
C accounts for VAT to Customs (£120 − £60)			60
Customer (D) pays	800	120	
Total of payments of VAT			120

Hence the customer pays £120 – the final tax is borne by the consumer. But the Customs and Excise picks up the tax as value is added at each stage of the business chain.

The government uses businesses as its tax collector for VAT. Just as with PAYE, the business person has to understand how VAT works and operate it. You should consult your accountant before your business gets underway to ensure that you administer the collection and payment of VAT correctly.

Before starting business you should contact your local VAT office. VAT offices are listed in local telephone books under 'Customs and Excise'. Ask the local office to send you their information about registering for VAT including 'The VAT Guide'.

Do I need to register for VAT?

If you are in *business* and make taxable *supplies*, the value of those supplies is called taxable turnover. If your taxable turnover exceeds £25,400 per year (1990 figure) you must register for VAT. Failure to notify your local VAT office within 30 days is an offence punishable by a fine. If you are registered, you are sent a VAT registration certificate with your VAT number on it. The number has to be used on all your invoices. The certificate should be kept safely. It is your proof of registration.

What is a 'business'?

VAT spreads its tentacles wide. For VAT, 'business' has a very wide meaning – it includes just about any continuing activity which is concerned with supplying goods or services to other people for a charge within the United Kingdom (this excludes the Channel Islands but includes the Isle of Man). If you make a charge but do not make a profit or aim to make a profit, you still have to register for VAT.

What are 'taxable supplies'?

Taxable supplies covers nearly all forms of business sales or supplies but excludes non-business activities, e.g. voluntary sales, jumble sales, etc.

Imports

VAT is charged when most goods are imported into the UK. There are certain exceptions, e.g. certain goods are relieved from import duties under EEC provisions. The VAT due on imports is paid directly to the Customs and Excise at the same time as any import duties have to be paid.

How VAT works

At the end of each accounting period (usually three months) each business has to make a VAT return to Customs and Excise. You have to understand the meaning of outputs and inputs. Outputs (as its name implies) describes goods or services going out from your business, i.e. sales. Inputs (again, as the name implies) describes goods or services brought into your business, i.e. purchases. The return shows

- the cost of all 'outputs' (before VAT), i.e. the price charged for the supplies of goods and services during that period to its customers;
- the cost of all 'inputs' (before VAT), i.e. the price paid for goods imported and goods and services supplied to it for the purposes of the business;
- the amount of VAT charged on 'outputs' – called 'output VAT';
- the amount of VAT paid on 'inputs' – called 'input VAT'.

A typical return would be as shown in figure 2.

You must keep all the tax invoices you have received which prove your inputs. A tax invoice will show

the purchase price for the goods/services
the VAT thereon
the supplier's VAT number

You cannot claim as an input any purchases on which you have not paid VAT, e.g. from a non-VAT registered supplier – the carpenter who works only for cash. Equally you must keep all your sales invoices to prove your outputs.

VAT rates – zero rating

The current VAT rates are 15 per cent and zero. Zero rating is good news. The government likes certain things and therefore encourages them via the VAT system. If you make zero-rated supplies

- you get credit for your input tax (see next section),
- you do not charge VAT on your outputs,
- this means that you can recover your input VAT from Customs and Excise.

Examples of zero-related supplies include (this is not an exhaustive list)

Value Added Tax Return
For the period
01 01 90 **to** 31 03 90

Registration number | Period
| 03 90

You could be liable to a finacial penalty if your completed return and all the VAT payable are not received by the due date.

Graeme Flash
T/A 'Bedazzled'
24 Bash Street
Sidcup

Due date: 30 04 90

| For official use |

Before you fill in this form please read the notes on the back.   Complete all boxes clearly in ink, writing 'none' where necessary. Don't put a dash or leave any box blank. If there are no pence write "00" in the pence column. Do not enter more than one amount in any box.

		£	p
VAT due in this period on **sales** and other outputs	1	1305	00
VAT reclaimed in this period on **purchases** and other inputs	2	783	00
Net VAT to be paid to Customs or reclaimed by you **(Difference between boxes 1 and 2)**	3	522	
Value of **outputs** (pounds only) excluding any VAT	4	8695	00
Value of **inputs** (pounds only) excluding any VAT	5	5217	00

Retail schemes. If you have used any of the schemes in the period covered by this return please enter the appropriate letter(s) in this box.

If you are enclosing a payment please tick (✓) this box.	DECLARATION by the signatory to be completed by or on behalf of the person named above.
	I, ...declare that the
	(Full name of signatory in BLOCK LETTERS)
	information given above is true and complete.
	Signature...Date ....19 ....

VAT 100   CD1942/N1(8.89)   F3790(JANUARY 1990)

Figure 2

150

exports
food
books, newspapers, magazines, music and maps
fuel and power (businesses pay 15 per cent VAT but domestic users do not)
drugs, medicines

VAT rates – exempt from VAT

Being exempt from VAT may sound like a good thing. In fact it is much less favourable than zero rating. If you are exempt from VAT you cannot claim credit for your input VAT. Hence VAT spent in an exempt business on purchases of equipment, fuel and power, office supplies is wasted. In effect VAT is a hidden tax cost on exempt businesses. The following are examples of VAT exempt business.

Insurance
Finance
Education
Health

Note: A small VAT exempt business cannot avoid input VAT on its VATable purchases.

The administration of VAT

If you have to register for VAT, the rules vary slightly depending on whether your business is established as a sole trader, partnership or limited company.

- A sole trader registers for VAT in his/her name.
- A partnership has to complete Form VAT 2. Registration may be in the firm's name or the partner's names. If partners change, the VAT commissioners must be notified within 30 days.
- A former partner is treated as a continuing partner for VAT purposes until his retirement is notified.
- Limited companies can have a 'group' registration which covers all companies in the same group, i.e. a holding company and its subsidiaries.

VAT returns

Most businesses registered for VAT have to make quarterly returns. Obtain the pamphlet 'Filling in Your VAT Return' from the local VAT office. The return must be submitted to the VAT office together with a cheque for any VAT due within one month of the end of each VAT quarter. So if you have to submit VAT returns on 31 March, 30 June, 30 September and 31 December, the VAT return must be submitted and any VAT paid by 30 April, 31 July, 31 October and 31 January. Failure to deliver a return and/or pay VAT due can give rise to a fixed scale of penalties. The penalties are based on the number of failures to furnish returns to pay VAT in the previous two years. The prescribed rate is

Number of previous failures	Daily penalty, the greater of
None	£5 or ⅙% VAT due
1	£10 or ⅓% VAT due
2	£15 or ½% VAT due

If you misdeclare VAT due by more than 30 per cent or £10,000 or 5 per cent of the total VAT due (whichever is the greater) you can be charged a penalty equal to 30 per cent of the VAT misdeclared.

Control

The government uses businesses as its unpaid tax collectors to collect VAT. It is not surprising that it has wide powers to check that VAT is being collected properly.

The normal method of VAT audit is the 'control visit' by the VAT man. Most control visits are made by prior appointment. This is a concession. The VAT commissioners have full power to walk in to business premises at any reasonable time. They can

- inspect and check the operation of a computer;
- inspect the premises and any goods found on them;
- demand production of documents, inspect and copy them or remove them 'for a reasonable period'.

You can demand to see the VAT man's identification.

The commissioners have wide powers if they consider there has been a breach of the VAT legislation. They can

- distrain (seize) goods;
- sue for overdue VAT in the High Court or county court;
- use attachment of earnings orders (see chapter 10);
- set off amounts due to the trader against amounts due from him;
- petition to bankrupt an individual or wind up a limited company (see chapter 11).

With a search warrant issued by a magistrate, the VAT commissioners can search premises and seize goods. Their powers of enforcement are much wider than the Inland Revenue's and are redolent of continental systems of government which is not surprising as VAT is a 'European' tax, first adopted by the French.

Key points

- Make sure your accounting systems and records are kept in a proper manner and up to date.
- Pay tax when it is due – using the government as a banker can work from time to time but it is not a sensible strategy to follow generally.
- Choose an appropriate financial year end.
- Be aware of the tax implications of the different types of organization: sole trader, partnership or limited company.
- Be cautious about treating people as self-employed.
- Tax can be a frightening subject. It combines complexity and tedium but cannot be ignored.

9

Dealing with the professions

Outline

You will almost certainly need good professional advice long
before you start trading. This chapter explains:

- what solicitors and accountants do
- how to choose them
- how much their professional advice will cost
- how to instruct them

The new business person will almost certainly have to deal with at
least two different professionals – his solicitor and his accountant.
He may, in addition, need to engage a surveyor to survey premises
or negotiate a rent review or a patent agent to register a trade mark,
a registered design or a patent. In each case he needs to know how
best to deal with them and what he can expect.

Solicitors

There are some 60,000 solicitors in England and Wales practising in
a great variety of ways, from in-house solicitors in big industrial
companies to one-partner firms to the massive City of London firms
with 150 or more partners. How does the new business person select
a firm from this great choice?

Choosing a solicitor

It is very important that you find a solicitor who knows what he is
doing; different firms specialize in different areas of the law. It is no
good going to a high street practice which specializes in divorce and

crime for advice on setting up a business. But equally the would-be entrepreneur, mindful of every pound he spends, will not want to go to one of the very expensive City firms. You need a suitable firm, but how to find it? And within each firm how do you find the right person to do your work?

1 The Law Society does not recommend solicitors or advise on their specializations. However, you can telephone the Law Society and ask for details of their 'Lawyers for Enterprise' scheme. This entitles you to a free consultation with any solicitor who belongs to the scheme and is aimed at those who are already running a small business or who are thinking of doing so. The Law Society (see appendix 2) keeps a list of participating firms. You could also get the list from enterprise agencies, other business advice agencies and town halls. Under the scheme you can have an initial free consultation with a solicitor who specializes in law affecting small businesses. He should advise you on how to establish your business, be it as a sole trader, partnership or limited company; about commercial property and indeed most of the subjects covered in this book. He will be able to give you an idea of what the legal costs involved will be. By using the scheme you should be able to find a local solicitor who has the specialisms you need.

2 You could talk to friends or acquaintances in your trade or line of business to see if they recommend anyone. It can be very useful to have a solicitor who understands the customs and practices of a particular industry.

3 You could talk to your bank manager and see if he knows of any local firms or can find out about any from the bank's network of contacts.

4 You could see if any firms advertise any relevant skills – solicitors are allowed to advertise (although not many do) but there are great limitations on advertising claims to specialization or particular expertise. So a solicitor cannot advertise 'tax law expert' or 'small business law expert' unless he is a member of a specialist Law Society panel. The best guide for the new business person would be to see if a solicitor advertises that he is a member of the 'Lawyers for Enterprise Scheme'.

5 You can talk to your trade association or local enterprise agency to see if they can make any recommendations.

Can the solicitor deal with my affairs?

Having found a firm, do not be shy about checking whether or not it can do the type of work you have in mind. Ask the solicitor what sort of work he does. Ask too what work the other partners in the firm do; how big the firm is; whether the solicitor will be assisted by anyone and, if so, by whom. Solicitors' firms are becoming specialized, so that both the major firms in provincial cities and the major London firms have specialized departments dealing with the law relating to companies, commerce, property, litigation as well as, in some cases, intellectual property, European matters, tax, franchising, consumer credit, etc. The small business person, just starting up, may find such a degree of specialization too great for his needs as it means that he may need to see one partner about corporate law, another about property and possibly a third concerning commercial matters such as terms and conditions of business. This becomes expensive. When thinking about choosing a solicitor it is worth bearing this in mind; you may be better off, at least initially, with a more general solicitor able to advise on all aspects of your business, albeit that he will not be able to advise to the same depth as a real specialist in any particular field.

If a new business does require specialist advice, say on tax, solicitors have access to the Bar. The barristers' monopoly of pleading cases in the High Court has attracted much public criticism and the Courts and Legal Services Act will allow solicitors to plead cases in the High Court but subject to certain restrictions. However, barristers serve a very useful function over and above their court work; they give advice on what is called non-contentious work, i.e. work that does not involve going to court. Many barristers are very specialized and through them solicitors are able to augment their own knowledge and skill. Due to the accidents of history, barristers occupy very cheap premises in London owned by the Inns of Court (the governing bodies of different groups of barristers). The low rentals and overheads paid by barristers result in their charging (by and large) rather less than solicitors. Hence the independent Bar allows solicitors to give their clients a rather more specialist service than the immediate resources of the firm might permit.

Solicitors' costs

Many people are both frightened by the possible charges and reluctant to ask how much the charges might be. You should not be; solicitors are quite accustomed to explaining their charging rates. What they will charge depends on a number of factors.

1 What is the hourly charge out rate? This varies enormously. A senior partner in a City firm could charge £250 per hour plus VAT. An assistant solicitor in a provincial firm might charge £50 per hour plus VAT. But do not be seduced by the cheapest price. Someone who charges a high rate may really know what he is doing and get the job done rather more quickly (and hence possibly more cheaply) than someone cheaper but less experienced who may labour long over what is to an expert a simple job.
2 Is the hourly rate the only basis of charge? Solicitors are entitled by *law* to charge more than the hourly rate. The Solicitors' Remuneration Order 1982 lays down that solicitors should charge a 'fair and reasonable' sum having regard to all the circumstances of the case and in particular to

- the complexity of the matter or the difficulty or novelty of the questions raised;
- the skill, labour, specialized knowledge and responsibility involved;
- the time spent;
- the number and importance of the documents prepared or perused;
- the place where and the circumstances in which the business or any part thereof was transacted;
- the amount or value of any money involved;
- the importance of the matter to the client.

As you can see time spent is but one of seven elements to be taken into account. This allows a solicitor to add on to or 'mark up' the time charge. You should therefore ask if the time charge is the only basis for charging. Will the solicitor give an estimate? If so it is not binding on the solicitor unless it is in writing and signed by both solicitor and client – it is then a fixed fee. Such arrangements are rare. Most solicitors are not prepared to commit themselves to a fixed fee as they have no way of knowing in advance how a particular job is going to turn out although they will often give an estimate.

Fees for leases

Certain jobs may be charged on a fee scale. The most important for the new business person is the scale applied to commercial leases, especially because the tenant is normally forced to pay the landlord's solicitors' costs as well as his own. The landlord's solicitor may well charge the scale fee.

Solicitors' bills

Solicitors use confusing jargon when talking about their charges; here is a brief guide:

Legalspeak	*Meaning*
Disbursements	Moneys paid by the solicitor to third parties in the course of carrying out the client's instructions, e.g. company registration fees, court fees
Profit costs	This is a total misdescription. It means the solicitor's fee, but the fee is *not* a profit. Out of the charges received the solicitor has to pay his overheads, staff costs, etc. Only after deducting all these items is he able to calculate a profit. Hence more modern-minded solicitors use the more accurate expression 'fees'
'Fee note'	Bill/invoice

A solicitor's fee note will consist of disbursements, fees and VAT.

How often will he bill me?

Many solicitors have a dreadful reputation for billing months or even years after the work has been completed. Contrary to expectations most clients hate this – they like to know where they stand rather than being hit two years later by a bill relating to work done in a period for which they have already drawn up accounts. If you want to be billed regularly (for example, quarterly) make this clear.

Instructing a solicitor

Once you have decided which firm you wish to instruct and found out how much they will charge you, you need to instruct the firm. Whatever the matter, be guided by a few simple observations:

1 A professional is not a clairvoyant; a qualified solicitor does not automatically understand your problems by virtue of his qualifications – many clients expect solicitors to be able to understand the intricate and complex details of their case (with which they have been labouring night and day) in a matter of moments and are then disappointed when the solicitor displays customary human frailties.
2 Give clear, well organized, instructions.

If you are instructing a solicitor on a long-running dispute, bring copies of all the documents and correspondence arranged in date order in a file, with a synopsis of the key matters at the front. If you dump a pile of unsorted papers in a great mess on his desk, he will spend valuable time (at your cost!) just sorting out the papers, trying to understand what has happened. If you are instructing him about a new business, bring details, again properly filed and organized, of your business plan and a list of the questions you want answered and the matters that need addressing.

Many of these points apply to instructing accountants, surveyors or other professionals.

What happens if you consider you have been overcharged by a solicitor?

A solicitor's fee must be 'fair and reasonable', taking into account all the circumstances. If you think a bill is unreasonable you should raise the matter with the solicitor straight away – it is rather difficult to query a bill which you have been sitting on for six months. You should discuss the fee with the solicitor and see if he is willing to reduce it. If he is not then you can

1 pay the full bill; or
2 not pay and ask the solicitor to submit his bill to the Law Society for them to check if the fee is 'fair and reasonable'; this only

applies to non-contentious work, i.e. not involving court work; for the client this is a good system as

- there is no fee payable, and the solicitor cannot charge for the extra costs incurred in submitting his files to the Law Society and getting a remuneration certificate;
- the Law Society can only reduce the bill or uphold it at its present level; the Law Society cannot increase it; the client cannot lose.

But note the following.

1 The procedure can take six months, whilst valuable papers are caught up at the Law Society.
2 The client must either ask for a remuneration certificate himself or *must* request the solicitor to obtain a remuneration certificate within one month of the solicitor giving him formal notice of his rights to obtain a certificate. If the request is not made within the one month period, the right to apply for a remuneration certificate is lost, although the client can still apply to the High Court and ask for the bill to be taxed, i.e. checked by a court official. The court can, like the Law Society, only uphold or reduce the bill but cannot increase it. The problem with taxation is the costs of the taxation – the court will order one of the parties to pay these. If the bill is reduced by less than 20 per cent the client usually has to pay; if it is reduced by more than 20 per cent, the solicitor pays. Solicitors cannot commence legal proceedings for recovery of outstanding fees without first giving the client written notice of his right to ask for a remuneration certificate from the Law Society. The solicitor cannot start the court proceedings for one month after the date on which the client was given notice of his rights. So the client must act promptly if he wishes to exercise his rights. The notice itself will often be somewhat oblique, e.g. 'You have the right under para (i) of Article 3 of the Solicitors' Remuneration Order 1982 to require us to obtain a certificate from the Law Society and there are provisions in the Solicitors Act 1974 relating to taxation of costs'.

The notice need say nothing about the one-month period for lodging a claim or precisely what the Solicitors Act 1974 says about taxation (verifying) of costs. So if you get a notice you have to respond quickly.

Money on deposit

Solicitors are also bound by rules on holding client's money. The Solicitors' Accounts (Deposit Interest) Rules 1988 provide that solicitors must pay interest to a client on moneys held by them as follows:

- over £500, interest after eight weeks;
- over £1,000, interest after four weeks;
- over £5,000, interest after two weeks;
- over £10,000, interest after one week.

The rate of interest has to be equivalent to a bank or building society's normal deposit rate.

Contentious (i.e. court cases) costs

In court cases the general principle is that the loser pays the winner's legal costs. Simple. But in reality complicated, as there are different methods of working out legal costs.

Most losers are ordered to pay costs on a 'standard basis'. This means that the loser only has to pay the costs which the winner 'reasonably incurred'. The loser gets the benefit of the doubt on the question of whether or not costs were reasonably incurred. The winner's costs are taxed or verified by a court official called a taxing master. If he rules that the client saw his solicitor too often he will disallow those costs. Thus the loser may well end up being ordered to pay only a part of the winner's legal costs. The winner will have to pay the difference. So the winner is not fully indemnified for his costs.

In a few cases where the loser's conduct has been unmeritorious, oppressive or in contempt of court, the winner's bill will be taxed on 'the indemnity basis'. This is basically the same as the standard basis but the winner gets the benefit of doubt on questions of whether costs were reasonably incurred.

In some cases the winner will *not* be awarded costs. These are

- when the winner did not deserve to win, e.g. in libel cases where 1p damages are awarded because although the judge considers the winner has won technically, he disapproves of the win;
- in small cases worth less than £500;
- where the loser had previously made a fair offer of settlement and paid a sum into court; if the court award is less than the sum paid into court, the winner will end up paying for all the legal costs arising since the date of the payment into court; hence payments into court can be a useful tactical weapon in litigation.

Complaints against solicitors

You should also know that the Law Society operates a complaints bureau to handle complaints against solicitors. It only *investigates* complaints. It does *not* investigate allegations of negligence. It does not make awards of compensation. The bureau investigates the complaint and has the power to call for the solicitor's files and papers. It can refer a matter to an adjudication committee which can recommend

- that disciplinary proceedings be brought – this can lead to a solicitor being struck off the roll and ceasing to be able to practice;
- that the solicitor be rebuked;
- that the solicitor submit progress reports.

If a complainant is dissatisfied with the way in which his complaint is being investigated he can complain to an investigation committee which is *not* dominated by solicitors.

If you think your solicitor has been negligent, you should instruct another firm of solicitors to act on your behalf. You need to be aware that some solicitors are very reluctant to sue their local fellow professional. You may be well advised to instruct a firm in a different town or area. Solicitors by law have to carry professional indemnity insurance to cover their liabilities for breach of professional duty or other obligations, so that if you do have to sue a solicitor, unless your claim is bigger than the limit of indemnity under his professional indemnity policy you will be dealing with his professional indemnity insurers.

Accountants

The accountancy profession has expanded remarkably over the past 150 years and especially in the last 15. As eloquent proof of Mark Twain's adage that 'there are lies, damned lies and there are statistics', a 1989 survey showed that, given the current expansion of accountants, by the year 2070 the entire working population of the United Kingdom will be employed as . . . accountants!

The initial growth of accountants was due to the requirements of the Companies Acts that each company incorporated under the Acts had to have its financial books and records audited or checked each year so that its balance sheet and profit and loss account gave a 'true and fair view' of the state of the company's affairs. The persons authorized to carry out such audits are now laid down by the Companies Act 1985. They include

- members of the Institute of Chartered Accountants in England and Wales;
- members of the Chartered Association of Certified Accountants.

Most accountants are members of the Institute of Chartered Accountants (known as the ICA but not to be confused with the Institute of Contemporary Arts which uses the same acronym).

In this chapter, all my comments about accountants refer to chartered accountants.

What accountants do

Accountants have shaken off their initial dependence on audit work. Although this remains a crucial part of their practice, all accountancy firms give advice on tax and estate planning and many have moved into management consultancy, advice on office systems, computerization, financial and management accountancy and even (writes a solicitor!) legal work. Like solicitors, but even more so, some firms of accountants have become enormous. The largest firms are members of world-wide partnerships with thousands of partners throughout the world and hundreds in the United Kingdom. Some of them are household names, in a way that no firm of solicitors is.

But just as with solicitors there are also small and medium sized firms which may well suit the new business person better.

Do I need an accountant?

If you are establishing a limited company, its accounts have to be audited. Therefore you need an auditor. If you are setting up as a sole trader or in partnership, you do not need an auditor. As mentioned in chapter 1, you merely need to submit (unaudited) accounts to the Inland Revenue. If you are registered for VAT your records have to be kept according to guidelines laid down by HM Customs and Excise. If you operate PAYE you have to keep proper records. But who is going to prepare those accounts? If they are based on back-of-the-envelope financial records will they be acceptable to the Inland Revenue or the VAT man? Answer: 'no', with the result that you could spend weeks painfully trying to re-create your financial records to their satisfaction and to the almost certain detriment of your business.

So however you establish your business it is wise to appoint an accountant. This applies even if you are employing an in-house bookkeeper. And it is wisest to consult your accountant, before you start trading, about how you should keep your financial records. The accountants will have to audit those records if you are a limited company or prepare accounts from them if you are not. If you keep them in a way that the accountants do not understand and they have to spend time fathoming them out, the costs of the audit will be much higher. It is therefore best to agree with your accountant what information you are going to keep and how you are going to maintain that, be it manually or on computer. Make sure the accountant understands what you are doing. Get him to come and inspect your embryo books, records, computer programs, etc., so that there can be as little room as possible for dispute later on the grounds of 'I never realized I had to do that', 'You never told me you were accounting on a cash basis rather than on a bills rendered basis', etc. He could also help you on payment of National Insurance contributions, value added tax and the operation of PAYE.

If you need tax advice, accountants have practical experience, as they deal with the Inland Revenue and VAT Commissioners on a regular basis.

How do I find an accountant?

You may already know of one or two firms because, as mentioned, some firms have a national and international reputation. But just because you have heard of a firm does not mean you should use them. Many of the points listed earlier about finding a solicitor are equally relevant to choosing an accountant.

Like the Law Society, the ICA will not recommend a particular firm of chartered accountants, nor does it publish a directory of firms listing their specialization, although it will give a list of firms practising in a locality on request. The ICA will supply you with a list of the 22 local district societies of Chartered Accountants and the committees of those local district societies may run schemes similar to the Law Society's 'Lawyers for Enterprise'. The ICA itself does not run anything comparable, but most firms of chartered accountants will give an initial interview free of charge. You need to ask about this when you ring up to make an appointment.

Instructing an accountant

The same general principles apply to instructing an accountant as apply to instructing a solicitor.

Disputes over fees

The ICA does not run a system like the Law Society's remuneration certificate procedure. Instead, if a client disagrees over an accountant's fee, he and the accountant can jointly agree to go to arbitration. If one party refuses, there can be no arbitration. The President of the ICA will appoint an independent accountant as arbitrator. The arbitrator will charge for his work (unlike the Law Society). The arbitrator decides who should pay his bill, whether it be one or other, or if they should share the cost. Accountants can sue for their fees. Again, unlike solicitors there are no restrictions on this.

Complaints

If you have a complaint about a Chartered Accountant you should write to the ICA Professional Conduct Department, 399 Sibury Boulevard, Central Milton Keynes MK9 2HL.

If a complaint is not resolved between the parties it will be referred to the ICA's investigation committee. The committee has power to refer the matter to a disciplinary committee whose powers range from a rebuke through a fine to being struck off the register of chartered accountants.

You can sue an accountant for negligence or breach of professional duty in the same way as you can sue a solicitor.

Conclusion

Having a good relationship with professional advisers is an important element in a business's success. A good relationship is not a subservient one. Remember that the Japanese economy thrives with a proportionately much lower number of professional advisers than in the UK. One theory of economic analysis claims that the prosperity of an economy is an inverse proportion of the number of lawyers to the total population. As the number of lawyers increases so prosperity wanes, and vice versa.

So do not run to your professional advisers every time you have a small problem. It'll cost you. Do use professionals when you really need them or when you have to, but be sparing and discerning – there is a good supply of useful material on many topics, some of which has been mentioned in this book.

Key points

- Find a solicitor who is skilled in business matters.
- Get your accountant involved early on.
- Always give your professional adviser a clear set of instructions.

10

Litigation

Outline

This chapter shows how you can sue in the county courts. It covers:

- tribunals
- letter before action
- particulars of claim
- who and where to sue
- the trial
- small claims

Naturally we hope that you will have nothing to do with the courts, unless it is in connection with something necessary for your business such as obtaining a liquor licence. But if you wish to sue someone or are sued yourself, it is important that you understand how the Court system operates.

Jargon

Litigation is littered with jargon but the following are some common expressions:

Jargon	*Meaning*
Action	A case which one person brings against another
Case	Another word for action
Defendant	The person against whom a civil action is brought

Injunction	An order of the court either restraining someone from doing something or ordering them to do something
Levying execution	Enforcing a court order
Plaintiff	The person who brings a civil action
Suit	Also known as 'law suit'; means the same as case or action
Summons	An order to appear before the court
Writ	An order to appear in the High Court – often used interchangeably with summons

Tribunals

In an attempt to get around the costs, formality and complexity of court cases many tribunals have been established to deal with cases quickly and cheaply. Because of this, legal aid is not available for tribunal work, even though in reality tribunal hearings are frequently lengthy and concerned with legal arguments. Tribunals are subject to control by the courts so that they must act fairly and properly – and some decisions on points of law can be appealed. Despite the hope that tribunals would be 'lawyer free' and hence dispense cheap and quick justice, this has not happened. Lawyers are, for example, frequently engaged to appear in industrial tribunals.

Do-it-yourself legal action

In many cases it is not wise to try to handle court proceedings without expert help. The rules of the various courts are many and complex; county court rules are different from the High Court and Court of Appeal; practice and procedure is hard to pick up from a book. For example, you should not try to handle injunction cases yourself – these have to be dealt with swiftly and a small hiccup over procedure could cost you dear. If your business is set up as a limited company then it has to instruct a solicitor to act on its behalf in connection with High Court litigation, although a representative can appear on behalf of the company in the county court.

The next sections show you how to handle a simple action to recover a debt. This would take place in the county court. The procedures described apply equally to other types of county court proceedings, so these sections are still worth reading. Debt recovery actions can be handled by the non-lawyer quite easily. If the defendant puts up a good defence, e.g. relating to quality of work done or brings a counterclaim (i.e. starts suing the plaintiff) it would be sensible to take professional advice.

How do I handle my own litigation?

Letter before action

First of all write what lawyers call 'a letter before action', i.e. write and claim the debt. To get round the persistent plea that 'I did not receive the bill or any of the reminders', send the letter before action by recorded delivery post. If it does not get delivered it will warn you early on that you may have problems finding the defendant. Your letter should state how much is due, and since what date, and that you are giving the defendant 14 days within which to settle the debt, otherwise you will commence proceedings in the county court for its recovery. Make sure you keep a copy of your letter and any enclosures.

Particulars of claim

If you get no reply or your debt remains unpaid, prepare particulars of claim. This is a summary of your claim. Make sure it is typed or written in block capitals in black ink. The particulars should contain the following information.

1 A heading with the name of the court and a space for the case number which will be allocated when the summons is issued.
2 Your name and address and also the defendant's (see later in this chapter for further details).
3 A brief statement of the facts of your claim and the money claimed.

The following is an example of the statement of facts.

1 On . . . day of . . . 19 . . . the Defendant agreed to buy goods to the value of £ . . . from the Plaintiff.
2 The said goods were delivered to the Plaintiff but the Defendant has failed to pay invoices numbered . . . in respect of the goods.
3 The Plaintiff claims:

   (a) £ . . . being the sum due in respect of the outstanding invoices.
   (b) Interest under Section 69 of the County Courts Act 1984 at the rate of . . . per cent per annum from . . . (the day of supply of the goods) to . . . (the date of the Summons) being £ . . . and thereafter interest at the same rate up to the date of judgment (see later in this chapter).
   (c) Costs.
   Dated this . . . day of . . . 19 . . .
   Signed . . .   who at this address will accept service of all pleadings and documents on his own behalf.

You can also add, if wished,

   (d) If the claim is disputed the Plaintiff applies for the proceedings to be referred to arbitration (see later in this chapter).

Interest

Unless interest is claimed in the particulars of claim it cannot be claimed at the trial. Hence it is worth claiming. The rate specified in the example is known as the court rate, and the county court will be able to tell you the current rate.

Who do I sue?

The defendant must be named correctly and the proper address used. If you are suing a business you must ask yourself the question: 'what type of business is it?' Back to chapter 1! Is it a limited company? Or a sole trader or a partnership? Or what?

Check the defendant's notepaper. This should show if it is a limited company, sole trader or partnership and give an address. If you are uncertain you can go through the following procedures.

1 Check in the telephone directory to see how the business is described.
2 Ring up a firm of company formation agents or law agents (look up under that heading in the *Yellow Pages*) and ask them to search at Companies House for the company's name *and* registered office. If no limited company is registered, the business must be conducted as a sole trader or partnership (unless it is an industrial and provident society, which is akin to a limited company but registered with the Registrar of Friendly Societies; they are very unusual and hence can probably be safely ignored).
3 Inspect the premises yourself.

Armed with the above information you can then bring your claim.

Sole trader

You sue the sole trader under his personal name. So Graeme Flash trading as 'Bedazzled' will be sued as 'Graeme Flash'. Make sure you get the correct address. This can be checked in the telephone directory or in the electoral register at the town hall. You do not have to use the trading address – the home address will suffice.

Partnerships

You must either sue the firm under its name or name all the partners. So Elias, Smith and Jones trading as 'The Comedy Partnership' must be sued either as 'The Comedy Partnership' or you must name all of Elias, Smith and Jones on the writ. Again, get the correct address.

Limited companies

You sue the company, not the directors or managers. You must state the correct registered office.

Where do I sue?

At this point 'justice's rule of maximum inconvenience' applies. As plaintiff and innocent party you cannot use the county court which is most convenient for you. You have to sue either in the court for the area where the defendant carries on business or the court for the area where the cause of action arose. For example, your business is in Norwich. You stay in a hotel in Brighton and get food poisoning. The registered office of the Brighton hotel is in London. You can sue in Brighton or London, but not Norwich.

The defendant has the right to have the case transferred to his local county court. So if you start proceedings in London, the salmonella-infected hotelier could switch the case even further away from Norwich – from London to Brighton.

Starting proceedings

Armed with your particulars of claim, properly completed as above, you can start court proceedings to recover your debt. You should send or take to the relevant county court

- form N201 available from county courts (free), 'Request for Default Summons';
- two copies of the particulars of claim;
- court fee; paid in cash or a crossed postal order payable to the 'Paymaster General' (cheques are *not* accepted); check what the current fees are;
- an envelope addressed to yourself.

Note that you should keep copies of all documents.

The court will issue a plaint note which sets out the case number and a summons. The plaint note will be sent to you to confirm that proceedings have begun. Always use the plaint number whenever you contact the court. The court will serve the summons on the defendant by post. If the letter is returned undelivered, the court will tell you. If that happens it's 'find your defendant time'! In other words, it will be up to you to find where the defendant has gone. You could hire investigators to seek him out.

Judgment in default

If by 14 days after service of the summons the defendant has done nothing, you are entitled to ask the court to enter what is called 'judgment in default' against the defendant. To do this you send the court

- form N30 (obtainable free from the court);
- the plaint note.

You must include the calculation of interest (if you claimed interest) on the form N30. You can ask that the defendant pay up the entire debt at once or by instalments. If you are uncertain about his ability to pay, it is best to ask for payment by instalments.

The court then issues judgment in your favour. You have to 'enforce' it (see later in this chapter).

The defendant admits the claim

When the court sends the defendant the summons, it also sends him a form of admission, defence and counterclaim. If the defendant admits the claim but wants time to pay he must answer questions about his financial position and can make an offer for payment. The court will tell you of the offer. You have 14 days within which you should tell the court whether or not you accept.

If you do not accept the offer of payment, the court will fix an appointment when the registrar will decide how the debt is to be paid. These appointments are called 'disposals'. You should attend. If you do not, you should write to the registrar with your proposals. If you do neither, your action may be struck off or adjourned. At the appointment you can quiz the defendant about his financial position. The registrar will then decide how the debt is to be paid, e.g. by one lump sum or by instalments. You may well be disappointed. The instalments ordered by the registrar may be very low. The courts operate on the principle that debtors frequently do not honour instalments and that a small, realistic sum is better than an over-ambitious one which is not met. If it is not paid you will then have to enforce payment.

The defendant denies the claim

To deny the claim the defendant must fill in the defence section of the admission, defence and counterclaim form sent to him with the particulars of claim by the court, and return it to the court within 14 days of service of the summons. You will be sent a copy of the defence.

Then come the next stages.

Pre-trial review

The court fixes a preliminary hearing – the pre-trial review. Practice varies about this. Some courts fix the date when they send the plaintiff a copy of the defence. In other courts the plaintiff (or defendant) has to apply for an appointment. The pre-trial review is an informal meeting at the court to sort out the necessary preparations and orders for the full hearing. You should take with you all relevant paperwork (bills, receipts, letters, etc.) to prove your case. If the defendant does not turn up you can apply for judgment in default of defence there and then. If you have the necessary proof, the registrar may award you judgment.

If the defendant does attend, the registrar will check the papers and, if he considers the particulars of claim are not clear or do not give enough information, he may ask the plaintiff for more details. He may then do the same with the defendant's defence. If either party needs further information from the other he should say so.

The registrar can order

- either the plaintiff or the defendant to give further and better particulars of the claim or the defence (as the case may be);
- the supply of relevant documents to the other party (e.g. invoices, copy letters).

The trial

The court fixes a date for the trial. Make sure the date is convenient for you. If you are to be on holiday on that date you can ask for another date. If you actually take your case to trial, you should follow these procedures:

1 Go and visit the court and sit for a couple of hours to observe how cases are conducted; how the judge is addressed ('Your Honour') and to take in the atmosphere so that you are not too put off when you go there for your case.
2 Evidence: bring any witnesses you can who will back up your case – a letter from a witness is not sufficient (save in arbitration cases). Your witnesses must give their evidence on oath and will be questioned by your opponent and the court. If a witness will not attend, you can force him by asking the court for a witness summons which you can get a bailiff to serve.
3 The trial:

- This takes place in open court – members of the public can sit in and hear the proceedings.
- You and your witness state your claim and give evidence first.
- The defendant can cross examine (i.e. question) you and your witness.
- The defendant and witness give evidence.
- You can cross examine the defendant and his witness.
- You and the defence can make a closing speech.
- The judge will then give judgment. The winner should ask for his costs to be paid by the loser. If the claim is for no more than £500, costs will not be awarded.

Small claims

Contrary to popular myth there is no 'Small Claims Court'. But there is a small claims procedure in the county courts whereby claims for less than £500 will be settled by arbitration. This is different from the trial procedure set out above. Special rules apply for arbitration. Cases for more than £500 can be heard by arbitration, if both parties agree.

1 You still have to start proceedings, as set out above.
2 An appointment will be fixed for hearing the dispute unless the parties agree that the arbitrator can make his decision based on papers and written statements submitted to him.
3 The hearing is informal and in private. So instead of being in the

public courtroom, it is conducted in a room, with all parties seated around a table.

4 The arbitrator will run the hearing as he thinks convenient and should give each party a fair and equal opportunity to present his case.

5 If one of the parties does not appear at the hearing the arbitrator may make an award having heard any other person who may be present.

6 An award made by the arbitrator in the absence of a party may be set aside. The absent party has to make an application for a fresh hearing, so whether or not this will be granted depends on the court.

7 An arbitrator may consult an expert for his views or commission a report on the matters in dispute.

8 Costs: no solicitor's costs on claims for less than £500 will be allowed except for

- the court fee for issuing the writ; and
- the costs of enforcing the award; and
- any costs certified by the arbitrator as having been incurred because of the unreasonable behaviour of the defendant in relation either to the proceedings or the claim.

The small claims procedure is very useful for small cases under £500 and can be used as well for claims over £500 if you are prepared to waive the balance over £500 and only claim £500, or if both parties agree to have the case dealt with by arbitration.

What happens if the defendant does not pay?

Winning a court case or an arbitration does not mean that you will automatically recover damages or the debt owed. The judgment merely confirms that the money is owed. If the defendant still does not pay up, then the plaintiff has to go back to the court and set in train yet more proceedings to ask that the court 'enforce' its judgment. Remember before you embark on this stage that the court cannot get blood out of a stone. If the debtor is penniless, teetering on the edge of bankruptcy or just adept at moving around, the court probably will be unable to assist successfully.

Remember, however frustrated you may feel, do not take the law into your own hands. It is a criminal offence to harrass a debtor into paying up a debt by

- falsely suggesting that the debtor could be prosecuted for not paying;
- falsely claiming to be an official or having an official document to enforce judgment;
- making demands which are calculated to subject the debtor or members of his family or household to alarm, distress or humiliation.

Can the defendant pay?

If you obtain a judgment in your favour you can ask the court to assess the defendant's financial position. Application has to be made to the county court for the district in which the defendant resides or carries on business. Usually this will be the court where you obtained judgment but it will not necessarily be and if necessary you will have to get the original court to transfer the proceedings to the new court (see later in this chapter).

If the defendant is a limited company you may examine a director, secretary or any officer. In the case of a firm, you can examine any of the partners. The examination takes place in private at the court and is conducted by a senior court official. There is a useful list of questions to ask, mainly aimed at personal rather than business debts, in the pamphlet 'Enforcing Money Judgments in the County Court', which is available free from all county courts.

If the debtor fails to attend the examination, you can apply for a new date to be set and for the debtor to be called before the judge. The notice warns the debtor that he may be sent to prison if he does not attend at the rearranged hearing. At the rearranged hearing the debtor first has to explain his non-attendance to the judge and the financial examination then takes place.

Enforcing the judgment

If the debtor does not comply with the court order to pay, you do not need to go through the rigmarole of examining his financial position. That may only cause delays while other creditors pile up judgments against him or his business. It is therefore sensible to try to enforce a judgment as quickly as possible. You must bear in mind, when reading this section, that the courts do not always move very quickly and enforcement can be a very slow process.

You can enforce a judgment in the following ways.

Send in the bailiff

The bailiff is an officer of the court. The creditor who has obtained a judgment applies to the court and asks for 'execution'. Use form N4(1), the plaint note, and pay a fee (15 per cent to a maximum of £38). This means that the bailiff will 'levy execution' against the debtor's goods, i.e. he will go and seize goods.

However, beware:

- The bailiff can enter premises by day or by night but not on Sunday.
- He cannot break into domestic premises but may break into premises used solely for business.
- He can only seize the debtor's property, so debtors always claim assets are owned by their wives or are on lease. This illustrates why it can be useful to examine the debtor *before* sending in the bailiffs – you can quiz him about what goods are on HP.

Note, however, that county court bailiffs have a poor reputation for success – they are easily put off. You should tell them as much as possible about the debtor's assets, e.g. if you know he owns the family car and not his wife – tell them.

The bailiff 'impounds' the goods and, if the debt is not paid off within five days, then the goods are sold at auction. Often the bailiff does not remove the goods. Instead the debtor signs a 'walking possession' agreement which entitles the bailiff to re-enter the premises at a later date to remove the goods. The debtor cannot sell goods that are subject to a walking possession order.

Garnishee proceedings

Another mystical legal title, 'garnishee', has nothing to do with garnishing salads. It comes from an Italian word meaning 'to warn'.

Under garnishee proceedings the creditor can apply to the court for an order that if someone owes money to the debtor he can be ordered to pay this debt to the court or so much of it as is required to pay the creditor. Most debts can be 'attached' in this way, but it is most normal to obtain money that is held in the debtor's bank account.

This can be a useful procedure but is little used because of the practical difficulties of finding out the details of sums owed to the debtor or of his bank account. Some companies do (very obligingly!) quote the name and address and details of their bankers on their payment demands or terms and conditions of business. You must complete form 4 (iii) and pay the court fee (£12.00).

Getting a charging order

If the debtor owns any land, a house or flat or securities (government stock or shares in a company), you can apply for a court order to charge them. To apply for a charging order you must swear an affidavit – drafting this can be difficult and it would at this stage be sensible to consult a solicitor. If the debtor still has assets worth charging, it will mean that he may ultimately be forced to pay up and you should be able to recover your legal expenses as well.

Charging orders on securities (shares, etc.) are usually very rare, as most debtors get rid of their assets well before creditors have resorted to court proceedings.

Obtaining a charging order on land is difficult as you have to be able to prove that the debtor does actually own the land in question. If you do not know whether or not he does own the land, you may check at the Land Registry which is now open to the public.

Attachment of earnings

This is the simplest to obtain and most common form of enforcement order. However it is of no use in business to business situations where business A owes business B money. It is used so that regular deductions are made from a debtor's pay by his employer and so the debt is paid off. Obviously it only works if the debtor is employed. If he is out of work or moves jobs a lot, an order will be useless.

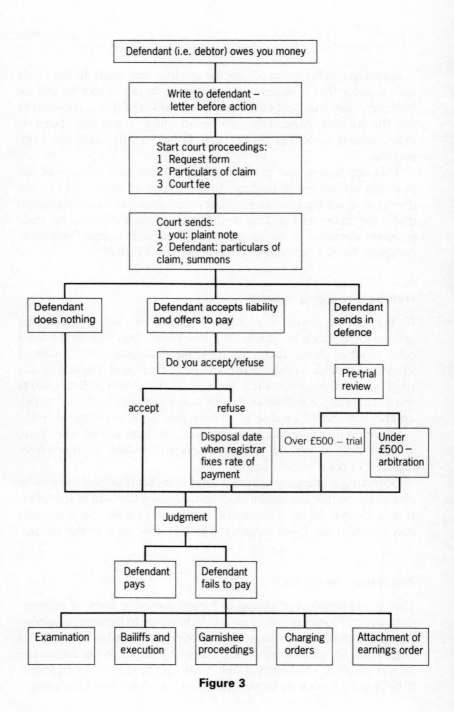

Figure 3

Summary

County court proceedings for the recovery of a debt can be summarized as shown in figure 3.

If you need further details about do-it-yourself litigation in the county court, a useful pamphlet entitled 'Small Claims in the County Court' is available, free, from county courts.

Conclusion

You should be aware of your limitations. DIY litigation should be fine for recovering simple debts in the county courts. If you are faced with more complicated litigation than that, you should consider consulting a solicitor. If you do, bear in mind the points made in chapter 9.

Remember too that most litigation is over non-payment of debts. If people do not pay up, it normally means one thing: they are in financial difficulties. Many other people may be pursuing them for money as well. It is therefore advisable to act quickly so as to get in as high up the queue of creditors as possible. Get your writ in fast and follow it up vigorously. But if the debtor goes bankrupt or (being a limited company) goes into liquidation first, the county court judgment in your favour will be of no use. You will still be an unsecured creditor, lining up with all the other creditors hoping to get something from the wreckage.

Key points

- Write a letter before action.
- Arbitration is recommended for small claims.
- Use DIY in the county court for debt recovery.
- Just because you get judgment in your favour does not mean that you recover your debt.
- Enforcing judgment may be difficult.
- Always act swiftly.

11

Insolvency

Outline

If your business fails, you will need to know how to handle it.
This chapter examines:

- personal bankruptcy
- receiverships
- company liquidation
- protecting your assets

As regularly as leaves fall off trees, businesses fail. Failure is an
integral part of capitalism. A number of well-known business people
have failed with their first and second ventures only to succeed
finally with their third. This may be of little solace to the business
person struggling to keep his business afloat – but is none the less
true! In 1989, 8138 people were made bankrupt in England and
Wales and 10,884 limited companies in England, Wales and
Scotland went into insolvent liquidation.

Sliding towards trouble

There are stages on the way to bankruptcy or insolvency. They start
with the cash flow problems – 'Can't pay; won't pay'. You string out
the creditors: Inland Revenue, VAT, landlord, trade suppliers,
professional advisers. Juggling creditors is difficult. You must keep
your trade contacts going to keep you supplied with stock and raw
materials so you aim to keep them sweet. The VAT man has
draconian powers and is not to be messed around.

Landlords have powers all of their own and have to be treated
very carefully when the cash is tight. Landlords can 'exercise

distraint' (also known as 'distrain') for unpaid rent and service charge. In plain English it means a landlord has the right to come into a tenant's premises and grab any of his assets (other than tools of trade). The landlord can then sell the seized assets and set the proceeds of sale off against the unpaid rent. If you're nervous about this happening, remember a landlord cannot break into occupied premises – only unoccupied ones and you can refuse him entry unless he has a court order. So if you're worried about the landlord sneaking in at night and whipping your stock – sleep on the job.

Your business may recover from its cash flow problems. Debtors may pay up. You land a big contract. But on the other hand the noose may get tighter. It may no longer be possible to juggle the creditors. Some may be about to enforce court judgments against your business to pay up outstanding debts. The bailiffs may be hovering. The VAT man may slap a walking possession order on your stock. The bank may be writing stiff letters and talking about enforcing its security. You may feel as if you are running from fire to fire. At this point you need to know about the various alternatives.

- *Bankruptcy* – if you are a sole trader or partnership.
- *Voluntary agreements* – if you are a sole trader, partnership or limited company.
- *Receivership* – if your business is a limited company.
- *Winding up* – if your business is a limited company.
- *Administration orders* – if your business is a limited company.

The effect of a business failure varies depending on how your business was structured. Failure hits sole traders and partnerships differently from limited companies. The sole trader or partners in a partnership who cannot pay their debts can be made bankrupt. A limited company is put into liquidation.

Definitions

Bankruptcy and insolvency law has its own special jargon. Here is an explanation of the more commonly used words.

Jargon	*Meaning*
Bankrupt	A person who has had a bankruptcy order made against him

Creditor	A person who is owed money
Debtor	A person who owes money
Insolvent	Unable to pay debts when they are due
Insolvency practitioner	A specialist in insolvency law, duly authorized by the Department of Trade and Industry, via the Institute of Chartered Accountants, the Law Society and other professional bodies
Liquidation	The controlled termination of a limited company; synonymous with winding up
Trustee in bankruptcy	A person who collects in the bankrupt's assets on behalf of the creditors; he will be either the official receiver or a qualified insolvency practitioner

Bankruptcy

It is not a criminal offence to be a debtor although it used to be. But to be declared bankrupt still has serious implications.

What is bankruptcy?

Bankruptcy is a way of dealing with your financial affairs if you cannot pay your debts. Bankruptcy proceedings are intended to

1 free the debtor from an overwhelming situation and enable him to make a fresh start;
2 make sure that the debtor's available resources are fairly distributed amongst the creditors; the debtor's assets are collected in by the trustee in bankruptcy.

How can you be made bankrupt?

The sole trader or partner does not have the protection of limited liability. If the business

- owes £750 or more and fails to pay this within three weeks of receipt of a statutory demand; or
- fails to satisfy a judgment debt

a creditor can apply to the court for an order of bankruptcy. This will be given if the court is satisfied that the debtor is unable to pay the debt or if there is no reasonable prospect of paying the debt.

Alternatively, a debtor can himself apply to be made bankrupt if he is being hounded by creditors and cannot pay his debts.

The court will issue a bankruptcy order if it is satisfied the debtor is bankrupt. But it will *not* issue an order if

- the debtor has paid the sum demanded in the statutory demand; or
- the court is satisfied that the debtor made the creditors a reasonable offer which has been unreasonably refused.

The effects of a bankruptcy order

As soon as a bankruptcy order is made, the debtor becomes an undischarged bankrupt. After public examination, all his or her property is vested in the official receiver who is a government official as trustee in bankruptcy subject to certain exceptions (see last section). Remember, this means all the debtor's personal wealth in the case of a sole trader or a partner. There is no distinction between your private wealth or assets and your business assets.

This merging of business debt and private assets is very important. It runs right through the law of bankruptcy. It is the best reason for starting a business as a limited company. But it is not always possible to get away with starting up as a limited company. You may have to give a personal guarantee, to back up or 'secure' the obligations of a limited company. And if you fail to honour a demand under the guarantee, if it exceeds £750, the person to whom the guarantee has been given, e.g. the bank, can in theory apply to the court to have you made bankrupt.

The official receiver then calls a creditors' meeting. The creditors can appoint their own trustee in bankruptcy. They will do this if they feel that the debtor may have assets which have been secreted away and feel that a private trustee may be more remorseless in his pursuit of the debtor than the official receiver. The bankrupt must

- prepare a statement of affairs for the trustee in bankruptcy within 21 days of the bankruptcy order;

- give the trustee all information required relating to his property, assets, etc.;
- protect and deliver his assets to the official receiver;
- notify his trustee of any property or increase in income obtained by him during his bankruptcy.

An undisclosed bankrupt cannot

- act as a director or be involved in the management of a company;
- be an MP, councillor or JP;
- obtain credit of £250 or more without revealing that he is an undischarged bankrupt;
- whether directly or indirectly, engage in any business under a name other than that in which he was adjudged bankrupt without disclosing to all persons with whom he enters into any business that he is an undischarged bankrupt.

If an undischarged bankrupt receives or earns money, it belongs to his trustee in bankruptcy who will only allow him a modest amount of money to support himself and his family. The rest is taken by the trustee and put towards paying the bankrupt's debts. That is the bad side of bankruptcy. But it also means that the bankrupt no longer has a direct responsibility to individual creditors. They may not press him for payment. They have to deal with his trustee in bankruptcy.

What property can a bankrupt keep?

The trustee in bankruptcy is not allowed to take

- property held by the bankrupt in trust for someone else, e.g. a magazine may take in subscriptions in advance – the moneys paid for future issues do not belong to the trustee in bankruptcy but to the subscribers;
- property subject to retention of title clauses (see chapter 4 for Romalpa clauses); under such clauses title or ownership of goods does not pass until payment has been made, hence if a bankrupt holds unpaid stock subject to a retention of title clause, the trustee in bankruptcy will not be able to sell it for the benefit of the creditors;

- tools of the bankrupt's trade, clothing and bedding, household equipment, etc., to serve basic needs;
- the matrimonial home; if the property is in joint names, the trustee can get a court order to sell it but he will only be able to keep that portion of the net proceeds of sale as belong to the bankrupt; this can be an argument for putting the family home in your spouse's name; however, this can have implications should the marriage break up (and one in three marriages do). Moreover any such gift might be set aside. Even if the matrimonial home is not in joint names the spouse who is not bankrupt may apply to the High Court for an order to delay the trustee in bankruptcy obtaining possession of the matrimonial home.

Administering the bankrupt's assets

The trustee in bankruptcy administers the bankrupt's estate by getting in all his assets and selling them off. This means all the business assets (e.g. stock, fixtures, fittings, debtors, etc.) and the debtor's private assets (e.g. his car, books, piano, etc.). The assets go to paying off his creditors, once the costs of the trustee have been met. There is an order of priority for paying off the creditors.

1 The secured creditors are paid first, e.g. the bank who has lent money secured on a charge or mortgage over the house.
2 The preferential creditors are paid second:

- one year's PAYE; six month's VAT,
- one year's class I and class II NI contributions,
- four month's arrears of employee's wages.

3 The ordinary creditors are paid next – if there is no money they get nothing. If there is something, this is divided pro rata amongst the creditors so each will receive x pence in the pound. This is called a 'dividend'. This has nothing to do with dividends paid on shares (see chapter 2).
4 If the creditors are paid in full (this rarely happens), the deferred creditors are paid. This will include anyone who lent money to the business tied to a share of the profits.

How does bankruptcy end?

A bankrupt is automatically discharged two or three years after the date of the adjudication order. This only applies to a person who has not been bankrupt before in the last 15 years.

- A bankrupt will be discharged after two years if the court issues a 'Certificate of Summary Administration'. This will be possible where the debts were less than £20,000.
- In all other cases a bankrupt will be discharged after three years.

If you have been made bankrupt before in the previous 15 years, you can only apply for a discharge five years after the date of the current bankruptcy order. Even then the court may refuse or delay giving the discharge.

The discharge releases the bankrupt from all the debts which he owed at the date of the bankruptcy order other than those arising from fraud.

An alternative to bankruptcy

Before the Insolvency Act 1986 became law, it was not possible for a debtor to make a legally enforceable compromise with his creditors. Any one of the creditors could torpedo a compromise proposal. The new law set up what are called 'voluntary arrangements'. This enables a debtor to make an offer to his creditors (called a proposal) for the payment of part or perhaps even all of the debts over a period of time.

How is it done?

1 The debtor applies to the court for an interim order. This states that he intends to make a proposal to his creditors and names a qualified insolvency practitioner who will help to prepare it.
2 This freezes the position. It prevents bankruptcy or other proceedings being brought for so long as the court thinks fit.
3 The insolvency practitioner will report to the court on the proposal.
4 If more than 75 per cent by value of the creditors attending a creditors meeting approve the proposal, it will be binding on *all* the creditors who were notified.

5 The named insolvency practitioner or someone appointed by the creditors supervises the arrangement.

Thus a voluntary arrangement can allow a debtor to arrange an orderly moratorium or compromise with his creditors without having to suffer the stigma of bankruptcy. But it of course depends on his having sufficient available resources to be able to make a reasonable offer to the creditors. In 1988 there were 779 voluntary arrangements.

Receivership

Receivers are different from liquidators. Receivers are appointed by a debtor's mortgagees. Say you or your company has given a fixed charge over assets in favour of your bankers. If the borrower defaults on its obligations to the above, e.g. fails to repay the capital when demanded, the bank can appoint a receiver. So too, in the case of a limited company, if a floating charge crystallizes (see chapter 2).

Receivers are usually given wide powers by the legal charge granted to the lender. The receiver is empowered to step in and run the business and sell its assets for the benefit of the persons who appointed him. He is under a duty when selling off the debtor's property to take reasonable care to obtain a proper sale price. He must take proper steps to secure the best available price at the time of sale. The receiver owes this duty not only to the debtor but also to anyone who has guaranteed the debtor's indebtedness.

Limited companies and receivers

In the case of a limited company the effects of the appointment of a receiver are

- floating charges crystallize and become fixed (see chapter 2);
- the company's powers and the directors' authority are suspended in relation to the assets covered by the receivership;
- the company's employees are automatically dismissed (this only applies if the receiver is appointed by the court);
- existing contracts with the company only have to be carried out

by the receiver if they affect the goodwill of the company, but in other cases he can disregard them;
- the registrar of companies has to be advised;
- notice of appointment has to go on the company's notepaper.

Application of assets – receivers

The receiver has to apply the proceeds of sale of its debtor's assets in the following order.

1 Costs of selling the assets (e.g. auctioneer's fees).
2 Receiver's costs.
3 The debt owed to the person who appointed the receiver.
4 Preferential debts (see earlier in this chapter).

However, if the receiver is appointed under a floating charge, the preferential debts are paid out before the debt owed to the holder of the floating charge.

Limited companies

Winding up or liquidation

Limited companies are potentially eternal. So long as they remain solvent and their shareholders so wish, they can keep going for ever. Although there are a number of different ways in which companies can be wound up and for a number of different reasons, the most commonplace cause of corporate mortality is insolvency. The following sections only deal with insolvent winding up.

A limited company is deemed to be unable to pay its debts if a creditor leaves a demand for a debt of £750 or more in a certain prescribed form at its registered office and the company fails to pay the debt within 21 days of the date of the demand being left. You can purchase the necessary form of statutory demand from legal stationers. Note that you must leave it at the registered office. This means checking where the registered office is (see chapter 10) and obtaining proof of delivery (e.g. a signature from a member of staff, or the deliverer should swear an affidavit of service).

If a company is unable to pay its debts, an application can be made to the court for the company to be wound up. The application can be made by

the company
any creditor
various government officials

After a winding-up petition has been presented, notice of the petition has to be advertised – hence all those notices in the press announcing company winding-ups. One of the best legal jokes for years was that the death throes of capitalist companies were advertised in the Communist daily the *Morning Star* which had the cheapest rates for such advertisements.

Liquidation

Before a winding-up order is made the court appoints a provisional liquidator – this is invariably the official receiver. His job is to preserve the assets and stop anyone grabbing them. As soon as the winding up order is made

- all court proceedings against the company are 'stayed' (stopped);
- all employee's contracts are terminated;
- the directors are dismissed and their powers to act on behalf of the company cease;
- all notices, writing paper, etc. must state that the company is in liquidation.

The official receiver has the discretion to call a preliminary creditors' meeting. This meeting is often the most highly charged in all the liquidation process. It takes place whilst memories of the directors' claims – 'I'll pay you next week'; 'The cheque's in the post, honest'; 'I've got this big new job, everything's going to be fine' – are still ringing in the creditors' ears. It is the one chance for angry creditors to vent their spleen at the directors. If the company has some assets, it is usual for an insolvency practitioner from the private sector to be appointed liquidator in place of the official receiver.

The liquidator's job is to get in the company's assets and pay off the creditors. The order of payment is similar to that for receivers (see earlier in this chapter).

Wrongful trading

Liquidators also have powers under the Insolvency Act 1986 to chase directors of insolvent companies who have been guilty of 'wrongful trading'. This is a new concept designed to make the protections of limited liability less certain. The old comfort of 'I trade through a limited company so the creditors can go and whistle' is no longer true.

Wrongful trading applies if a company goes into insolvent liquidation. Insolvent means being unable to pay debts as they fall due. The liquidator of a company which has gone into insolvent liquidation can now apply to the court for an order that a director or officer or 'shadow director' (i.e. someone who was effectively a director) be ordered to make a contribution to the company's assets. In others words bang goes limited liability. Directors, officers and shadow directors can be made personally liable for an insolvent company's debts. How much do they pay? That depends on the court.

A director, officer or shadow director can be found guilty of wrongful trading if at some time before the company went into insolvent liquidation he knew or ought to have concluded there was no reasonable prospect that the company would avoid going bust. The courts apply an objective test in assessing whether or not a director knew or ought to have known whether the company would go under. It is no use the director claiming that he was thick, ignorant or only there for the best claret. A director's conduct will be compared with that of a reasonably diligent person having the general knowledge, skill and experience that might reasonably have been expected of a person carrying out the director's job as against the general knowledge and experience which that particular director had. One case has already sent shivers down the spines of directors. In *Re Produce Marketing Limited* (1989) former directors of an insolvent company found guilty of wrongful trading were ordered to pay £70,000 to the liquidator.

Fraudulent trading

If in a winding-up it appears that any business of the company has been carried on with intent to defraud creditors or for any fraudulent purpose, the court may declare that any of the directors who were knowingly parties to the fraud shall be personally liable for all or any of the debts of the company. No limited liability.

Misfeasance

Directors can also be ordered to pay back any money or property that they have wrongfully obtained or taken from an insolvent company.

Disqualification of directors

Former directors of insolvent companies can also be banned. You can be disqualified from becoming a director for up to 15 years although most bans are much smaller – only 11 people were banned in 1988 for more than 10 years and only 356 were banned in total in that year mainly for periods of between one and five years.

Disqualification orders must be made against a director of a company that was at any time insolvent if the court finds his conduct as director makes him unfit to be concerned in the management of a company. Disqualification orders may be made

1 if a director has been convicted of any criminal offence in connection with a company, e.g. fraud;
2 if the court considers a director has been guilty of fraudulent trading (see earlier in this chapter);
3 if the court orders a director to make a contribution because the company has engaged in wrongful trading;
4 if a director has been in persistent default in complying with the disclosure requirements of company law, e.g. filing annual returns and accounts.

Breach of a disqualification order can lead to a spell in prison, or a fine or both. Moreover you can also be made personally liable for the debts and liabilities of the company incurred when you were so involved. And it is no good staying in the background giving your spouse your orders. Whoever obeys your orders can be made personally liable themselves.

Administration orders

The Insolvency Act 1986 introduced voluntary arrangements to help individuals and limited companies to trade their way back from near bankruptcy. This Act also introduced legislation to help limited companies with similar problems. The law is detailed and complex. Very briefly, if a company is unable to pay its debts and if the court considers that an administration order is likely to achieve

1 the survival of the company and the whole or part of its undertaking as a going concern, or
2 a more advantageous realization of the company's assets,

it will make an administration order.

The administration order is granted after the court has considered a rescue plan from an insolvency practitioner and is satisfied that the rescue plan is feasible. If an administration order is made, it gives the company a breathing space during which time the administrator can attempt to revive the company. During the period of the administration

- the company cannot be wound up;
- no steps may be taken to enforce any security against the company or to repossess goods, save with the consent of the court;
- no other proceedings and no execution of legal proceedings and no distress (see earlier in this chapter) may be levied without the court's approval.

Administration orders offer the limited company which is faced with insolvent liquidation the chance of a period of respite and consolidation freed from the demands of its creditors. The crucial ingredient for obtaining an administration order is money. If the company has the cash available (either from shareholders or lenders) to finance a reorganization, then the court may well be satisfied that an administration order is appropriate. But if there is no cash, then administration will almost certainly not succeed. The number of administration orders made is small. In 1988, 198 were made.

What can I do to shelter my assets?

Many people's thoughts turn to protecting their personal assets when faced with the possible collapse of their business. If you have only traded through a limited company, given no personal guarantees and having nothing to fear from the fraudulent trading or wrongful trading law, then clearly you have no fears about personal liability. But if you are a sole trader, a partner or have given personal guarantees to support a limited company, what can you do to shelter your assets? Can you stick them in your spouse's/parents'/trustees' names and let the creditors go hang? Answer: 'no'.

The Insolvency Act 1986 has tightened up the law. If you are made bankrupt the trustee in bankruptcy may apply to the court to have set aside 'a transaction at an undervalue' (e.g. gift, sale for a price less than the true value) made within the five years prior to the petition. So giving away your share of the family home to your spouse six months before your business goes down will not save it from your creditors.

Worse still, even if you plan things well in advance, you may still have problems. Suppose you have assets which are not needed in your business, e.g. your house – this presumes you are not required to put that up as a security for a loan to your business. You decide to give away your house to trustees with you as a beneficiary of the trust. Or you give it to your spouse. At the time of the gift you and your business are solvent.

If subsequently you are sued for a debt or any other type of claim, whoever is making the claim against you can apply to the court to set aside the gift if you do not have the assets to meet the claim. The court will order the gift to be set aside if it is satisfied it was made for the purpose

1 of putting assets beyond the reach of a person who is making or may at some time make a claim against him; or
2 of otherwise prejudicing the interests of such a person in relating to the claim which he is making or may make.

The five-year rule does not apply in this case. Apart from these considerations, giving assets away also has effects on the division of assets in the case of divorce, on wills (who inherits?), etc. Hence approach giving-it-all-away-to-dodge-the-creditors, with care.

Conclusion

If your business is facing very serious financial problems, creditors outstripping cash and other assets, you may need to think about what bankruptcy and/or winding-up an insolvent company means.

Deciding to bury your business is invariably painful. Most people therefore delay doing it as long as possible, in the hope that something will turn up. And of course sometimes it does. But more often it does not. If you are beginning to have doubts about your business's capacity to survive, the best advice is to get professional assistance sooner rather than later, before you have run up even more debts. This may enable you to put together a voluntary arrangement or have an administration order made. It will certainly mean that there is less chance of your being pursued for wrongful trading or made bankrupt.

Key points

- Insolvency is preceded by many warning signs.
- Take note of the warnings and respond sooner rather than later.
- Giving your assets away does not always avoid liability.
- Bankruptcy hits individuals.
- Liquidation hits limited companies.

Appendix 1: Sources of information

Company law

Notes for Guidance – the Companies Act 1985
Notes for Guidance – the Companies Act 1985 Disclosure Requirements
Notes for Guidance – Sensitive Words and Expressions
Notes for Guidance – New Companies
Notes for Guidance – Company Names
Notes for Guidance – Striking Off, Dissolution and Restoration
Notes for Guidance on Business Names and Business Ownership
Notes for Guidance on Limited Partnerships
Notes for Guidance – Company Secretaries, Duties and Responsibilities

All the above can be obtained by writing to Companies House (see appendix 2) and asking for a set of their free *Notes for Guidance*.

Employment law

A series of pamphlets numbered 1 to 17 on

1 *Written Statement of Main Terms and Conditions of Employment*
2 *Redundancy Consultation and Notification*
3 *Employees Rights on Insolvency of Employer*
4 *Employment Rights of the Expectant Mother*
5 *Suspension of Medical Grounds under Health and Safety Regulations*
6 *Facing Redundancy? Time off for Job Hunting or to Arrange Training*
7 *Union Membership Rights in the Closed Shop*
8 *Itemised Pay Statements*
9 *Guarantee Payments*
10 *Employment Rights on the Transfer of an Undertaking*
11 *Rules Governing Continuous Employment and a Week's Pay*
12 *Time Off for Public Duties*
13 *Unfairly Dismissed*
14 *Rights to Notice and Reasons for Dismissal*
15 *Union Secret Ballots*
16 *Redundancy Payments*
17 *Limits on Payments*

You could also ask for the pamphlets about

Trade Unions – Trade Union Executive Elections PL866
Unjustifiable Discipline by a Trade Union PL865
Union Membership and Non-Membership Rights PL871
Industrial Action and the Law PL870 – *A Guide for Employers*
Industrial Action and the Law PL869 – *A Guide for Employees and Trade Unions*
Trade Union Political Funds PL868
Trade Union Funds and Accounting Records PL867

All the above are available free from ACAS or the Department of Employment local offices.

Health and Safety

Health and Safety pamphlets – Safety Committees.

Securing Compliance with Health and Safety Legislation at Work – Health and Safety Executive
An Introduction to the Employment Medical Advisory Service
Health and Safety at Work etc. Act 1974 – Your Obligations to Non-Employees
Time off for the Training of Safety Representatives
The Law on Health and Safety at Work – Essential Facts for Small Businesses and the Self Employed
Health and Safety Commission – The Health and Safety at Work etc. Act 1974 – the Act outlined

All the above pamphlets are available free from your local Health and Safety Executive Area Office.

Litigation

Small Claims in the County Court
Enforcing Money Judgments

Both of the above are available free from your local County Court.

Patenting

Patenting, the Opportunities and the Pitfalls
'Technology Transfer'

Both of the above and other pamphlets are available free from the British Technology Group.

Tax and National Insurance

A number of very useful pamphlets, etc. are available free of charge from the Inland Revenue and the DSS. Ask for the *New Employers Starter Pack* P4. Also useful are

IR28 – *Starting in Business*
IR57 – *Thinking of Working for Yourself?*
IR53 – *Thinking of Taking Someone On?*
IR34 – *PAYE*
IR71 – *PAYE Inspection of Employers Records*
IR69 – *Expenses Forms P11D*
IR56/IR39 – *Employed or Self Employed*
IR480 – *Notes on Expenses, Payments and Benefits for Directors and Certain Employees*

Trade Marks

'*Applying for a trade mark*'.

Free from the Trade Marks Registry, but somewhat out of date.

Value added tax

There are a large number of free publications available from the VAT office.

NB. 'Should I be registered for VAT?'
The VAT Guide
VAT Publications – This sets out a list of particular pamphlets on VAT which may be of relevance to you in your business

Appendix 2: Useful addresses

Advisory, Conciliation and Arbitration Services (ACAS)

Head Office
27 Wilton Street
London SW1X 7AX
Tel: 071 210 3000

London Region
Clifton House
83/117 Euston Road
London NW1 2RB
Tel: 071 388 5100

South East Region
Westminster House
Fleet Road
Fleet
Hampshire GU13 8PD
Tel: 0252 811868

South West Region
Regent House
27A Regent Street
Clifton
Bristol BS8 4HR
Tel: 0272 744066

Midlands Region
Alpha Tower
Suffolk Street
Queensway
Birmingham B1 1TZ
Tel: 021 631 3434

Nottingham (sub-office)
66/72 Houndsgate
Nottingham NG1 6BA
Tel: 0602 415450

Northern Region
Westgate House
Westgate Road
Newcastle upon Tyne NE1 1TJ
Tel: 091 261 2191

Yorkshire and Humberside Region
Commerce House
St Albans Place
Leeds LS2 8HH
Tel: 0532 431371

North West Region
Boulton House
17/21 Chorlton Street
Manchester M1 3HY
Tel: 061 228 3222

Merseyside (sub-office)
Cassington House
249 St Mary's Road
Garston
Liverpool L19 0NF
Tel. 051 427 8881

Scotland
Franborough House
123/157 Bothwell Street
Glasgow G2 7JR
Tel: 041 204 2677

Wales
Phase 1
Ty Glas Road
Llanishen
Cardiff CF4 5PH
Tel: 0222 762636

National Federation of Self-employed and Small Businesses

Head Office
32 St Anne's Road West
Lytham St Annes
Lancashire FY8 1NY
Tel: 0253 720911

London Office
140 Lower Marsh
London SE1 7AE
Tel: 071 928 9272

Scottish Development Agency

Edinburgh Office
Rosebery House
Haymarket Terrace
Edinburgh EH12 5EZ
Tel: 031 337 9595

Glasgow Office
120 Bothwell Street
Glasgow G2 7JP
Tel: 041 248 2700

Small Firms Service

Freefone Enterprise for all offices,
via operator (100)

Head Office
Department of Employment
Steel House
Tothill Street
London SW1H 9NF

London and South East Region
2nd Floor
11 Belgrave Road
London SW1C 1RB
Tel: 071 828 6231

Reading Office
Abbey Hall
Abbey Square
Reading RG1 3BE
Tel: 0734 591733

South West Region
6th Floor
The Pithay
Bristol BS1 2NB
Tel: 0272 294546

Northern Region
15th Floor
Calecross House
156 Pilgrim Street
Newcastle upon Tyne NE1 6PZ
Tel: 091 232 5353

North West Region
26–28 Deansgate
Manchester M3 1RH
Tel: 061 832 5282

Merseyside (sub-office)
Graeme House
Derby Square
Liverpool L2 7UJ
Tel: 051 236 5756

Yorkshire and Humberside Region
1 Park Row
City Square
Leeds LS1 5NR
Tel: 0532 445151

East Midlands Region
57 Maid Marion Way
Nottingham NG1 6GE
Tel: 0602 481184

West Midlands Region
9th Floor
Alpha Tower
Suffolk Street
Queensway
Birmingham B1 1TT
Tel: 021 643 3344

Eastern Region
Carlyle House
Carlyle Road
Cambridge CB4 3DN
Tel: 0223 63312

Stevenage Office
Business & Technology Centre
Bessemer Drive
Stevenage
Hertfordshire SG1 2DX
Tel: 0438 743377

Wales
16 St David's House
Wood Street
Cardiff CF4 1ER
Tel: 0222 396116

Scotland
120 Bothwell Street
Glasgow G2 6NR
Tel: 041 248 6014

Northern Ireland
Local Enterprise Development Unit
Ledu House
Upper Galwally
Belfast BT8 4TB
Tel: 0232 491031

Welsh Development Agency

Head Office
Pearl House
Greyfriars Road
Cardiff CF1 3XX
Tel: 0222 222666

South West Wales Office
Swansea Industrial Estate
Fforestfach
Swansea SA5 4DL
Tel: 0792 561 6666

General

Association of British Chambers of
   Commerce
Sovereign House
212a Shaftesbury Avenue
London WC2H 8EW
Tel: 071 240 5831

203

British Technology Group
101 Newington Causeway
London SE1 6BU
Tel: 071 403 6666
(Specialists in technology transfer
and advice on patents)

Business in the Community
227A City Road
London EC1V 1JU
Tel: 071 253 3716

Companies House
Crown Way
Maindy
Cardiff CF4 3UZ
Tel: 0222 388588

London Search Room
Companies House
55/71 City Road
London EC1Y 1BB
Tel: 071 253 9393

Companies House
100/102 George Street
Edinburgh EH2 3DJ
Tel: 031 2255774

Confederation of British Industry
(CBI)
Centre Point
103 New Oxford Street
London WC1A 1DU
Tel: 071 379 7400

Co-operative Development Agency
Broadmead House
21 Panton Street
London SW1Y 4DR
Tel: 071 839 2988

Council for Small Industries in Rural
Areas (CoSIRA)
141 Castle Street
Salisbury
Wiltshire SP1 3TP
Tel: 0722 336255

Data Protection Registration Office
Springfield House
Water Lane
Wilmslow
Cheshire SK9 5AX
Tel: 0625 535711

Department of Employment
Caxton House
Tothill Street
Westminster
London SW1H 9NF
Tel: 071 273 3000

Department of Trade and Industry
Financial Service & Companies
Division
10/18 Victoria Street
London SW1H 0NN
Tel: 071 215 5000

Department of Trade and Industry
Overseas Trade Divisions
1/19 Victoria Street
London SW1H 0ET
Tel: 071 215 5000

Development Board for Rural Wales
Ladywell House
Newton
Powys SY16 1JB
Tel: 0686 626965

Highlands and Islands Development
20 Bridge Street
Inverness IV1 1QR
Tel: 0463 234171

HP Information plc
(Marketing Department)
11 Grosvenor Gardens
London SW1W 0BN
Tel: 071 828 0851

HP Information plc
(all other depts except marketing)
PO Box 61
Dolphin House
New Street
Salisbury
Wiltshire SP1 2TB
Tel: 0722 413434

Industrial Common Ownership
    Movement Ltd
Vassalli House
20 Central Road
Leeds LS1 6DE
Tel: 0532 461737

Industrial Development Board for
    Northern Ireland
IDB House
64 Chichester Street
Belfast BT1 4JX
Tel: 0232 233233

Institute of Chartered Accountants
    in England and Wales
Chartered Accountants Hall
PO Box 433
Moorgate Place
Moorgate
London EC2P 2BJ
Tel: 071 628 7060

Institute of Directors
116 Pall Mall
London SW1Y 5ED
Tel: 071 839 1233

Institute of Small Businesses
13 Golden Square
London W1R 4AL
Tel: 071 437 4923

3i plc,
91 Waterloo Road
London SE1 8XP
Tel: 071 928 7822

Land Charges Department
Drakes Hill Court
Burrington Way
Plymouth PL5 3LP
Tel: 0752 779831

Land Registry
32 Lincoln's Inn Fields
London WC2A 3PH
Tel: 071 405 3488

Law Society
The Law Society's Hall
113 Chancery Lane
London WC2A 1PL
Tel: 071 242 1222

London Chamber of Commerce
69/73 Cannon Street
London EC4N 5AB
Tel: 071 248 4444

London Enterprise Agency
(LENTA)
4 Snow Hill
London EC1A 2BS
Tel: 071 236 3000

London Gazette
Room 403
HMSO Publications Centre
51 Nine Elms Lane
London SW8 5DR
Tel: 071 873 0011

Northern Ireland Local Enterprise
  Development Unit
Ledu House
Upper Galwally
Belfast BT8 4TB
Tel: 0232 491031

Office of Fair Trading
Field House
15/25 Bream's Buildings
London EC4A 1PR
Tel: 071 242 2858

Patent Office
State House
66/71 High Holborn
London WC1R 4TP
Tel: 071 831 2525

Registry of County Court Judgments
173/175 Cleveland Street
London W1P 5PE
Tel: 071 380 0133

Trade Marks Registry
State House
66/71 High Holborn
London WC1R 4TP
Tel: 071 831 2525

Head Offices of Wage Councils
Steel House
Tothill Street
London SW1H 9NF
Tel: 071 273 4812

Appendix 3: Business names

Part 1

The following words and expressions will require the consent of the Secretary of State for Trade and Industry before their use will be allowed in a company name. The words fall into the following categories:

1 Words which imply national or international pre-eminence

International
National
European
United Kingdom
Great Britain
British
England
English
Scotland
Scottish
Wales
Welsh
Ireland
Irish

2 Words which imply government patronage or sponsorship

Authority
Board
Council

3 Words which imply business pre-eminence or representative status

Association
Federation
Society
Institute
Institution

4 Words which imply specific objects or functions

Reinsurer
Group
Holdings
Post Office
Giro
Trust
Stock Exchange
Friendly Society
Industrial & Provident Society
Building Society
Trade Union
Foundation
Fund
Charter

Register	Chartered
Registered	Sheffield
Patent	Benevolent
Assurance	Patentee
Insurance	Chamber of Commerce
Reinsurance	Chamber of Trade
Reassurance	Chamber of Industry
Insurer	Co-operative
Assurer	Chemist
Re-assurer	Chemistry

Part 2

The following words and expressions also require the Secretary of State's consent and normally a company would be registered by a name containing any of the following words or expressions only if the applicant had obtained a letter of non-objection from the relevant department or body. Any correspondence should be submitted with the appropriate registration documents.

Word or expression	Relevant body for companies intending to have registered office in England or Wales	Relevant body for companies intending to have registered office in Scotland
Royal, Royale, Royalty, King, Queen, Prince, Princess, Windsor, Duke, His/Her Majesty	'A' Division (Rm 730) Home Office Queen Anne's Gate London SW1H 9AT	Scottish Home and Health Department Old St Andrews Hse Edinburgh EH1 3DE
Police	F1 Division Police Department Home Office Queen Anne's Gate London SW1H 9AT	Police Division Scottish Home and Health Department Old St Andrews Hse Edinburgh EH1 3DE

Word or expression	Relevant body for companies intending to have registered office in England or Wales	Relevant body for companies intending to have registered office in Scotland
Special School	Schools RN II Branch Dept of Education and Science Elizabeth House York Road London SE1 7PH	As for England and Wales
Contact Lens	The Registrar General Optical Council 41 Harley Street London W1N 2DJ	As for England and Wales
Dental, Dentistry	The Registrar General Dental Council 37 Wimpole Street London W1M 8DQ	As for England and Wales
District Nurse, Health Visitor, Midwife, Midwifery, Nurse, Nursing	The Registrar and Chief Executive UK Central Council for Nursing, Midwifery and Health Visiting 23 Portland Place London W1N 3AF	As for England and Wales
Health Centre	Division C34(B) Room B1205 Dept of Health Alexander Fleming Hse Elephant and Castle London SE1 6TE	As for England and Wales
Health Service	HS2D Division (Room 1115) Dept of Health and Social Security Hannibal House Elephant and Castle London SE1 6TE	As for England and Wales

Word or expression	Relevant body for companies intending to have registered office in England or Wales	Relevant body for companies intending to have registered office in Scotland
Nursing Home	Dept of Health Room A513 Alexander Fleming Hse Elephant and Castle London SE1 6TE	As for England and Wales
Pregnancy, Termination, Abortion	PMC2A Division Room B1210 Dept of Health Alexander Fleming Hse Elephant and Castle London SE1 6TE	As for England and Wales
Breed, Breeder, Breeding	Animal Health III Div Ministry of Agriculture Fisheries and Food Hook Rise South Tolworth Surbiton Surrey KT6 7NF	As for England and Wales
Charity, Charitable	Registration Division Charity Commission 14 Ryder Street St James' London SW1Y 6AH	Civil Law and Charities Division Scottish Home and Health Department St Andrews House Edinburgh EH1 3DE
Apothecary	The Worshipful Society of Apothecaries of London Apothecaries Hall Blackfriars Lane London EC4	The Pharmaceutical Society of Great Britain 1 Lambeth High Street London SE1 7JN
University, Polytechnic	FHE3 Dept of Education and Science Elizabeth House York Road London SE1 7PH	As for England and Wales

Part 3

The use of certain words in company names is covered by other legislation and their use may constitute a criminal offence (see Section 26(1)(d) of the Companies Act 1985). Some of these words are listed below but the list is not exhaustive. Applicants wishing to use any of these words may therefore be asked to seek confirmation from the relevant body listed that the use of the word does not contravene the relevant legislation. The Department of Trade and Industry also reserve the right to seek the advice in each case direct from the relevant body if necessary.

Word or expression	Relevant legislation	Relevant body
Architect, Architectural	Section 1 Architects Registration Act 1938	The Registrar Architects Registration Council of the UK 73 Hallam Street London W1N 6EE
Credit Union	Credit Union Act 1979	The Registrar of Friendly Societies 15/17 Great Marlborough Street London W1V 2AX
Veterinary Surgeon	Sections 19/20 Veterinary Surgeons Act 1966	The Registrar Royal College of Veterinary Surgeons 32 Belgrave Square London SW1X 8QP
Dentist, Dental Surgeon, Dental Practitioner	Dentist Act 1984	The Registrar General Dental Council 37 Wimpole Street London W1M 8DQ
Drug, Druggist, Pharmaceutical, Pharmaceutist, Pharmacist, Pharmacy	Section 78 Medicines Act 1968	Head of the Law Dept The Pharmaceutical Society of Great Britain 1 Lambeth High Street London SE1 7JN

Word or expression	Relevant legislation	Relevant body
Optician Ophthalmic Optician, Dispensing Optician, Enrolled Optician, Registered Optician, Optometrist	Sections 4 & 22 Opticians Act 1958 and Health and Social Security Act 1984	The Registrar General Optical Council 41 Harley Street London W1N 2DJ
Bank, Banker, Banking Deposit	Banking Act 1979	Bank of England Threadneedle Street London EC2R 8AH
Red Cross	Geneva Convention Act 1957	Seek Advice of Companies House
Anzac	Section 1 Anzac Act 1916	Seek Advice of Companies House
Insurance Broker, Assurance Broker, Re-Insurance Broker, Re-Assurance Broker	Sections 2 & 3 Insurance Brokers (Registration) Act 1977	Seek Advice of Companies House
Chiropodist, Dietician, Medical Laboratory Technician, Occupational Therapist, Orthoptist, Physiotherapist, Radiographer, Remedial Gymnast	Professions Supplementary to Medicine Act 1960 if preceded by Registered, State Registered, State	Room 77 Dept of Health Hannibal House Elephant & Castle London SE1 6TE

Glossary

administration order Court order under the Insolvency Act 1986 whereby a limited company can be reorganized during a period of court enforced tranquility.

administrative receiver A receiver or manager of a limited company's assets appointed under a mortgage, charge or floating charge or other security.

arbitration The settlement of a dispute by an independent third party chosen by the persons in dispute.

Articles of Association Rules setting out how a limited company's constitution is to be run; it regulates the internal affairs of the company.

attachment of earnings An order of the court that a debtor's debt be paid out of his earnings on a regular basis.

audit The process of checking the accuracy of financial records by an independent third party.

bankruptcy When an individual cannot pay his/her debts and is declared insolvent by court order; the individual's property thereafter is administered for the benefit of his creditors.

charge A deed given by a borrower or a guarantor to secure the repayment of his borrowings to the lender. It means the same as a mortgage.

counterclaim When a defendant is sued he can include in his defence any claim which he could bring against the plaintiff, even if it arises from another matter.

credit sale agreement Agreement for the sale of goods under which the purchase price is payable by instalments.

CGT Capital gains tax.

CT Corporation tax.

damages Compensation or indemnity for loss suffered which can be claimed in law.

distress   The act of taking goods out of the possession of a tenant by a landlord to compensate for non-payment of rent.

dividend   Share of profits paid to shareholders by a limited liability company.

execution   This has two meanings:

1 The act of completing or carrying into effect a judgment of the court.
2 The due completion of a deed in accordance with the law.

garnishee   A debtor in whose hands a debt has been attached, i.e. the debtor has been warned only to pay his debt to a person who has obtained a judgment against the debtor's own creditor.

garnishee order   The order served on a garnishee attaching a debt in his hands.

guarantee   A promise to answer for the debt or default of someone else.

guarantor   Someone who binds himself by a guarantee or who promises to answer for another's debt or liability; also known as a surety.

hire purchase agreement   Agreement under which the buyer can buy the goods or under which the property in the goods passes to the buyer at the end of the hire period.

indemnity   A promise to make good a loss suffered by another.

injunction   An order or decree of a court whereby someone is required to do or stop doing a particular thing.

insolvency   The situation in which a limited liability company or an individual or business is unable to pay its debts as they fall due.

joint and several liability   If A and B are jointly and severally liable to C, then C has three possible courses of action. He can sue either A or B or A and B. Hence severally means separately.

joint tenancy   When two or more people hold property as joint tenants they own it between them and if one dies the other takes his share automatically.

judgment creditor   Someone in whose favour a judgment of the court for a sum of money is given against a judgment debtor.

judgment debtor   A debtor who has had a court judgment for the debt made against him.

lessee   A person who takes a lease, i.e. the tenant.

lessor   A person who grants a lease, i.e. the landlord.

lien   The right to hold the property of another as security for the performance and obligation, e.g. a garage owner who holds a car until the repair bill is paid.

liquidated damages   A specific sum, e.g. £10, or a sum that can be easily worked out, e.g. 50 days interest at 10 per cent per annum.

liquidation   The process of closing down an insolvent limited company and realizing its assets to pay off its debts.

liquidator   The person who liquidates a limited company.

loan capital   Moneys lent to a business or limited company for a fixed period. It gives no share of profits.

memorandum of association   rules setting out what a limited company can do.

mortgage   A loan of money secured on property. The lender is the mortgagee and the borrower is the mortgagor.

negligence   An act or omission which causes damage allowing the person who has suffered injury to sue for compensation.

NI   National Insurance.

passing off   A civil wrong whereby X passes off his goods or business as being that of Y, e.g. by using a similar name, design or logo.

PAYE   Pay as you earn.

plaintiff   The person who sues or brings a civil action.

PLC   A public limited company.

pleadings   The formal written documents in a civil action. These constitute the statement of claim (issued by the plaintiff) and the defence (issued by the defendant).

premium   Under a lease a sum paid over and above the rent, e.g. leasehold office premises with 20 years left on the lease sold for £20,000 – the £20,000 is a premium.

rack rent   The full open market rent.

receiver   A person appointed either by a court or under a mortgage deed to take possession of an individual's or limited liability company's property and to sell it to satisfy debts.

registered office   The office of a limited liability company which is registered at Companies House.

reversion   If an owner of land disposes of it for a period after which it will go back to him, he is said to hold the reversion, e.g. a landlord grants a 100 year lease. He still holds the freehold reversion.

right of re-entry   The right of a landlord to take possession of premises if the tenant breaks the terms of the lease or tenancy.

secured creditor   A person whose debt is secured, e.g. by a mortgage or charge on property as security for a loan.

statute   An Act of Parliament.

strict liability   Automatic liability independent of fault on the part of the defendant.

summary judgment   If a defendant does not show an arguable defence to a claim, the plaintiff can apply for summary (i.e. quick) judgment.

surety   A guarantor.

tort   A civil wrong other than a breach of contract giving rise to the right to bring an action in the civil courts, e.g. for nuisance, defamation, negligence.

uberrimae fidei   Of the utmost good faith.

unlawful   An act is unlawful if it is a breach of the law and so permits civil proceedings to commence. It is not the same as a breach of the criminal law which is an illegal act.

unliquidated damages   Damages which cannot be calculated in advance and are dependent upon the views or generosity of the court, e.g. for the loss of a leg.

vicarious liability When one person is responsible for the actions of another because of their relationship, e.g. an employer is liable for the actions of his employee. A plaintiff can sue either or both.

winding up The operation of terminating a business by realizing its assets and settling its liabilities.

writ A document commencing a High Court action.

Barclays Guides for the Small Business

The following titles are available in this series:

Wilson: *Financial Management for the Small Business* 0 631 17254 8

Rogers: *Marketing for the Small Business* 0 631 17247 5

Aziz: *Computing for the Small Business* 0 631 17256 4

Wilson: *International Trade for the Small Business* 0 631 17252 1

Maitland: *Managing Staff for the Small Business* 0 631 17482 6

Lloyd: *Law for the Small Business* 0 631 17349 8

Stanworth & Smith: *Franchising for the Small Business* 0 631 17498 2

Gray: *Managing Growth in the Small Business* 0 631 17249 1

Gammon: *Buying and Selling for the Small Business* 0 631 17528 8

All titles are £6.95 each.

You can order through your local bookseller or, in case of difficulty, direct from the publisher using this order form. Please indicate the quantity of books you require in the boxes above and complete the details form below. The publisher will be pleased to negotiate a discount for orders of more than 20 copies of one title.

Payment

Please add £2.50 to payment to cover p&p.

☐ Please charge my Mastercard/Visa/American Express account

card number ☐☐☐☐☐☐☐☐☐☐☐☐☐☐☐☐☐☐

Expiry date _____

Signature _____

(credit card orders must be signed to be valid)

☐ I enclose a cheque for £_____ made payable to **Marston Book Services Ltd**

(PLEASE PRINT)

Name _____

Address _____

_____

_____ Postcode _____

Tel No _____

Signature _____ Date _____

Please return the completed form with remittance to:

Department DM, Basil Blackwell Ltd

108 Cowley Road, Oxford OX4 1JF, UK

or telephone your credit card order on 0865 791155.

Goods will be despatched within 14 days of receipt of order. Data supplied may be used to inform you about other Basil Blackwell publications in relevant fields.

Registered in England No. 180277 Basil Blackwell Ltd.